Fishing Camps

FISHING
CAMPS

RALPH
KYLLOE

GIBBS·SMITH
P
PUBLISHER

SALT LAKE CITY

For the mighty fish of the world. You've provided us with more pleasures than you'll ever know. You are some of God's finest creatures.

For old fishing friends Harry Salmen, Mike Beecher, Jack Gunter, and Rob Sulski—dear friends whom I don't see often enough. May we grow old gracefully and with a fishing pole in our hands. Tight lines.

First Edition
99 98 97 96   5 4 3 2 1

This is a Peregrine Smith Book, published by
Gibbs Smith, Publisher
P.O. Box 667
Layton, UT 84041

Text and photographs copyright © 1996 by Ralph Kylloe

Edited by Gail Yngve
Designed and produced by J. Scott Knudsen, Park City, Utah
Printed in Hong Kong

Library of Congress Cataloging-in-Publication Data

Kylloe, Ralph R.
    Fishing camps / Ralph Kylloe. -- 1st ed.
        p.   cm.
    "A Peregrine Smith book" --T.p. verso.
    ISBN 0-87905-757-2
1. Fishing--North America--Anecdotes. 2. Fishing lodges--North
    America--Guidebooks. 3. North America--Guidebooks.   I. Title
    Sh462.K95   1996
    799.1'0971--dc20   96-19258
                                CIP

FISHING GUIDES

During the past twenty years, I've had the opportunity to hire guides from many different areas around the country, and I will continue to do so. Fish are different in each area, and the guides are familiar with their own territories, which ultimately saves fishermen time and yields more fish. A good guide will always be honest enough to tell prospective customers if the fish are not biting.

In reality, hundreds of excellent guides can be found throughout the fisheries of North America. Unfortunately, space prohibits my listing them all here. Local bait shops are good places to inquire about the best guides in the area. Great guides will usually have references.

The guides listed here are a few I've hired year after year without disappointment.

John Oravec
14272 Oak Orchard River
   Road
Waterport, NY 14571
(800) 433-2510

John Leech
02442 Spring Lake Road
Fruitland Park, FL 34731
(904) 352-5724

Tony Hussey
8606 Southwest 2nd Street
Okeechobee, FL 34731
(800) 535-2113

Harry McDonald
632 Erickson Road
Campbell River, Vancouver Island
V9W 5N9 Canada
(604) 923-2236

Judd Weisberg
Route 42, Box 177
Lexington, NY 12452
(518) 989-6583

Keith Short
730 Cash Creek Drive
Jackson, WY 83001
(307) 733-8495

FISHERMAN'S PRAYER

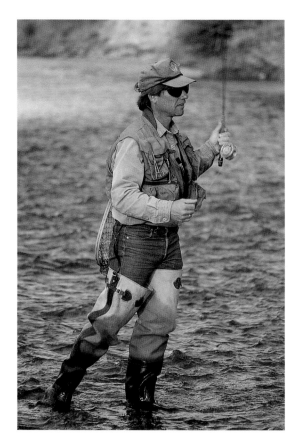

God grant me that I

may live to fish

until my dying day,

And when it comes to my last cast

I then most humbly pray.

When in the Lord's safe landing net

I'm peacefully asleep

That in his mercy I be judged

Good enough to keep.

CONTENTS

PREFACE

I have always loved the experience of fishing. So it was a natural thing for me to suggest to my publisher that I complete a book on one of the world's favorite pastimes. Initially I wanted to write and present photos of the fishing experience at various locations around the country. But as time went on, I fell head over heels in love with many of the traditional fishing camps found throughout North America. So I came to the conclusion that the idea of the book should be expanded to include many of the wonderful lodges and camps that cater specifically to the fisherman.

From the beginning I will categorically state that this book is far from complete in terms of fishing lodges and camps. In reality, no one person could possibly hope to fish all the waters across North America. It is my hope that sometime during the next few years I can spend a few weeks fishing and visiting the camps of Texas, the Southwest, as well as Wisconsin and Michigan. Hopefully, I can write about them in another book. However, I tried in this book. to present a geographic cross section of the major fishing areas around the country. I also wanted to present some of the historical information of North American fishing. I further sought to present a few personal anecdotes of my own fishing experiences as well as look at some of the fishing styles developed by local fishermen.

From the start I sought old places, places with a history or a sense of uniqueness that differentiated them from others. Often times the owners were so charismatic that their personalities and their relationship with their guests warranted the inclusion of their camp in this book. Such is the case with the Woodman House on Wolfe Island. Other times the decor and setting of a facility was so perfect and artistic that it would have been a crime to not mention it. Such was the case with the Crescent H Ranch in Wyoming. But I also wanted to include places where the owners and employees were friendly and congenial, places where I felt comfortable staying. The places listed here have some of the friendliest people in the world associated with them.

There are far too many people to thank than I can remember at this writing. I know that the moment this book comes off the press I will think of several more individuals who should have been acknowledged for their help. Nonetheless, a sincere and profound thank you goes to: Keith Short, John Leech, Tony Hussey, Gussy Pitts, Barbara and Thad Collum, Eric Christensen, Judd Weisberg, Terry and Sandy Winchell, Margaret Wood, Brian Clarkson, George Jaques, Bob Oestriecher, Margaret Grade, Christie and David Garrett, Kathryn Kincannon, Jack Gunter, Mike and Debbie Beecher, Harry Salmen, Rob Sulski, John Oravec and numerous others. A special thanks to my editor, Gail Yngve. Her help with this manuscript has been invaluable. Last but not least, a very special thanks to my wife and principal fishing partner, Michele, who indulges and tolerates me as we travel across the country searching for the "big one." As always this book would not have been possible without her!

INTRODUCTION

Often while fishing in a lake or stream, eyeing the diversity of life around me, I am reminded of man's origins and of our link to these simpler aquatic life forms. I believe this is the reason that we are drawn back to the water time after time.

Somewhere within us all is the genetic memory of the first life, formed after the earth's cooling some billions of years ago as the giant bodies of water pooled across the land. In time, a giant meteor slammed into the earth, carrying minerals that would eventually and miraculously combine to make life. First, tiny-celled microbes emerged; then, as the power of life surged forward, more powerful beings emerged, this time with strong backs and fins that allowed for exceptional movement and agility. After millions of years, our finned friends slithered onto land and eventually transformed themselves into an almost infinity of living creatures we could never have imagined in our wildest dreams.

FLY-FISHING GUIDE KEITH SHORT
OF JACKSON, WYOMING, CERTAINLY
ONE OF THE BEST GUIDES IN THE
ROCKY MOUNTAINS, CASTS A FEW
FLIES IN THE GREEN RIVER, JUST
EAST OF JACKSON.

Life was further added to waters at high elevation by ducks and their ability to fly. Fish, in a brilliant adaptation, produced a viscous, sticky substance that enclosed their eggs and stuck to the feet of ducks to be transported to faraway waters.

Like life everywhere, fish adapted to their circumstances and survived the most inhospitable of environments. Every ecological niche was filled, and species of unbelievable differences and abilities now filled the waters across the entire earth. No clean body of water was without their presence.

A few hundred thousand years ago, just a mere speck of time in relation to the extraordinary age of the cosmos, the earth, for the fifth time, tilted slightly off axis and brought unbearable cold to many regions across the globe. The fifth ice age the earth had seen brought mountains of crystallized water, miles thick, to cover the northern regions of earth. These glaciers rumbled across the land at a

A STEELHEAD TROUT CAUGHT IN WASHINGTON STATE.

Eventually, fish became divided into two categories—those living in the massive salty seas and those adapting to fresh waters. Life spread dramatically throughout the bodies of water that were now landlocked via the streams brought about by the unseen magnet of gravity.

A STRINGER OF TROUT PULLED OUT OF JACKSON LAKE YEARS AGO.

snail's pace and tore deep depressions in the landscape. As a result, mountains and valleys were left as scars upon the land. Nothing was sacred under the great weight of the glaciers that were driven, like all other objects on the planet, by gravity.

Eventually, the earth tilted back and warmth returned, causing the meltdown of many of the giant glaciers. Now, some ten thousand years after the last ice age, giant boulders are strewn across the land, and thousands of lakes dot the northern hemisphere— some so large we call them the Great Lakes and many so small they have yet to be explored and named. But the fish found them anyway.

In time, humans crossed the Bering Strait from China to Alaska. From there they headed south and east. Imagine, for just a moment, what it was like to walk from Alaska to New York and Florida and never see another human being, fence, or building, just unparalleled beauty. Herds of buffalo were uncountable, the skies so full of birds that they darkened the sun, and salmon so thick in the waters that you could almost walk across their backs to the other side of the bay without getting your feet wet.

Resourceful creatures, humans survived off both the land and water. They took no more than was necessary to keep themselves alive. In time, a great reverence evolved in humans for the land and waters that supported their very lives.

Much later, peoples from across the seas arrived and they, too, survived off the land and waters. In New England, lobsters were so plentiful that pilgrims could collect hundreds within a few hours and use them as fertilizer under each kernel of corn. On the West Coast, eighty-pound salmon could be pulled in one right after the other, and in the interior of the continent, fish were so plentiful

that they could be caught by hand or with simple spears.

As the Industrial Revolution progressed, great wealth was amassed and many individuals found time on their hands. Seeking a retreat from the travails of inner-city life, industrialists and business owners retreated to the countryside for sport, relaxation, and rejuvenation. In time, numerous retreats for both the wealthy and the middle class populated the wilderness, and many of these lodges and

A YOUNG GIRL PROUDLY DISPLAYS A STRINGER OF FISH.

CAMPING IN MAINE 6284

A MAINE
FISHERMAN AND
CAMPER FROM
ANOTHER ERA.

FISHING CAMP IN
NORTHERN NEW
ENGLAND.

retreats were created specifically for hunting and fishing.

Keeping in mind that humans first lived in caves and huts for thousands of generations, the owners of these new retreats kept tradition with our ancestors by decorating in the style of their forebears. This style included trophies of the hunt, artwork of the animals that were fished and hunted, fishing and hunting tools, fireplaces, and furniture made of natural materials such as antlers, logs, sticks, and roots.

Initially, great wilderness retreats were constructed in the Adirondack Mountains in the style of the hunting resorts of Europe and Scandinavia. Today, many of the same lodges still exist and are flourishing. Built at the turn of the century, facilities that covered thousands of acres dotted the Adirondack Park. In Keene Valley, wealthy New Yorkers built the Ausable Club that today operates as a marvelous

A CAMPING SCENE FROM MAINE.

A PROUD FISHERWOMAN WITH A MONSTER MUSKIE CAUGHT IN THE ST. LAWRENCE RIVER.

private fishing and recreational retreat.

In Old Forge, the Adirondack League Club encompasses fifty thousand acres and includes numerous lakes and streams. The League Club, founded more than a hundred years ago, still operates today as a private facility and maintains its own trout hatchery and three full-time biologists. Hundreds of other facilities, both large and small, as well as public and private, dot the park and take advantage of an area that once had "a fish on every cast and a moose behind every tree."

Just north of the Adirondack Park lies the St. Lawrence waterway. There, for more than a hundred years, fishermen have taken advantage of one of the most productive areas in North America. Dotted with thousands of small islands, the St. Lawrence River is the home of huge muskies and northern pike, large- and smallmouth bass of impressive quantity and quality, and game fish of all sorts. Fishing camps were first established there in the mid-eighteen hundreds, and today camps on Wolfe Island are on the National Historic Register. Numerous fishing contests are held on these waters yearly and a significant part of the economy is geared to the fishing

15

AN ANTIQUE
PHOTOGRAPH OF A
FAMILY FISHING
OUTING ON
RANGELEY LAKE,
MAINE.

ANOTHER
STRINGER OF
NORTHERN PIKE
CAUGHT IN THE
1920S.

industry. Bait shops, tackle stores, sport bars and restaurants, marinas, and fishing guides are all part of the local heritage. Worms, tackle, and other baits are sold in local grocery stores, laundromats, and liquor stores throughout the region.

Farther west, in the interior of Michigan, glacier-carved lakes and streams are the homes to a wide variety of fish that have been hunted since the turn of the century. Today, in the Baldwin area, numerous rivers and streams exist that serve as breeding waters for an impressive array of trout and salmon living permanently in Lake Michigan. Numerous fishing camps exist in both upper and lower Michigan that are filled to capacity with fishermen hoping to take advantage of a very impressive salmon and trout run during fishing season.

In Wisconsin, glacier lakes are found with great frequency. Like other areas of the country, a significant part of the local wilderness economy is based on the fishing experience, and literally hundreds of fishing camps, open in both winter and summer, are available at reasonable fees. Certainly the most interesting area is the town of Hayward in northern Wisconsin. The waters around Hayward are best known for muskie and walleye fishing, and the area offers numerous fishing-tackle shops, fishing museums, and celebrations geared toward the fishing experience.

Minnesota, The Land of Ten Thousand Lakes, is world renowned for the fishing experience. Certainly, the best known is the Boundary Waters Canoe Area, starting just north of Ely. This eloquent region is abundant with crystal-clear lakes, wildlife of all sorts, and spectacular fishing. The beauty of the area is enhanced by motorboats not being permitted in many areas of the park waters. Canoes are the only mode of transportation, which

ensures tranquility and an abundance of fish available only to those rugged enough to paddle, often for days, to get to the "promised waters."

Fishing became popular in the early and middle part of this century. Certainly increased

ICE FISHING IN NORTHERN WISCONSIN.

THIS CHILD SHOWS OFF A TROUT IN GRAND TETON NATIONAL PARK.

efficiency in transportation afforded access to many of the truly remote regions, and fishing fanatics from the cities of Boston, New York, Detroit, Chicago, and Minneapolis suddenly found that exceptional wilderness fishing spots were only a day or two's drive.

In the Rocky Mountains, trappers and mountain men were well aware of the extraordinary fishing opportunities from the beginning of the 1800s. Once the railroads progressed throughout the West, vast new areas were made available to sportsmen seeking new challenges. From the late Victorian period on, hundreds of dude ranches and retreats were constructed throughout the mountain regions, and sportsmen were elated at the large numbers of trout available in the cold mountain streams.

In and around Jackson Hole, Wyoming, numerous dude ranches sprang up and took advantage of many pristine rivers, including the Snake, New Fork, and Green Rivers.

Farther north in the newly discovered territory of Yellowstone Park, anglers delighted in rivers such as the Yellowstone, Madison, Firehole, and Slough Creek. Farther south near Aspen, Colorado, anglers took delight, as well as a fair share of trout, in Frying Pan, Roaring Fork, and Tagert's Lake. By the mid-1930s, the northern Rockies were home to some of the finest sporting ranches the country had ever seen. Guides were kept busy year-round, and customers were willing to pay any price for a week's horseback trek through the Rockies, catching monster trout and fighting with grizzly bears for the premier fishing spots.

Fishermen were treated to awesome scenery and first-class accommodations in such famous mountain retreats as the Spotted Horse Ranch just south of Jackson and the Crescent H Ranch just west of town. Both ranches were constructed in the 1920s and today still operate as first-class fishing resorts. The camps maintain a variety of wonderful log

cabins and are outfitted in traditional mountain camp decor with taxidermy and furniture made of elk antlers, with venison, duck, and freshly caught trout piled high on the dinner tables.

On the far West Coast of North America, fishermen were treated to certainly some of the finest big-game fishing in the world. Home of the world's most fearsome salmon, the waters from northern California to Alaska were rich with king, coho, and pink salmon as well as incredible steelhead and rainbow trout. Not only were game fish plentiful, but the waters off the coast were rich with killer whales, sea lions, otters, eagles, osprey, and an incredible diversity of other forms of wildlife.

At the turn of the century, fishermen flocked to these areas and fished for the mighty tyee king salmon weighing more than

A PAIR OF FISHERMEN WITH THEIR LUNCHES. IN THE EARLY DAYS OF FLY-FISHING, IT WAS QUITE COMMON FOR THE UPPER CLASSES TO WEAR TIES ON THEIR FISHING TRIPS.

thirty pounds. In time, the famous Tyee Club was formed in the Campbell River area of Vancouver Island. Membership was limited to individuals who landed a tyee from a motorless rowboat, using lightweight tackle and artificial bait. The club is still in existence today, and hundreds of hopeful fishermen make the yearly pilgrimage to Canadian waters in pursuit of companionship and the opportunity to do battle with some of the most powerful and exciting fish in the world.

From Northern California on up, hundreds of fishing camps cater to the aspirations of salmon fishermen. Some of these camps, such as Manka's Inverness Lodge in Inverness, California, are stunningly beautiful facilities decorated with their original antiques and tucked away in beautiful coastal towns. The quaintness, charm, accommodations,

delicious food, and hospitality of Manka's Lodge and many others like it ensure their full occupancy year-round not only by fishermen but adventure seekers in pursuit of folklore, a bit of history, and the ultimate weekend get-away.

Other facilities, such as Painters Lodge in Campbell River, British Columbia, are huge world-class resorts that employ numerous guides and cater to dozens of fishermen and their families at a single time. Other facilities in the Campbell River area include such high-class lodges as The Campbell River Lodge and April Point Lodge located on Quadra Island just off the coast of British Columbia. Both these facilities opened their doors in the 1930s and still maintain a significant historic presence. These lodges are world renowned for their high-class, personal ambiance as well

as their authentic rustic mode, fishing, facilities, and scenery.

Farther down the coast in sunny California, fishermen take great delight in the hundreds of bodies of water located throughout the interior of their state. World-record bass have been caught in many of their lakes, and their area is certainly known for its stunning scenery. Hundreds of facilities are available to those who bother to explore the wilderness areas. Numerous bass-fishing contests are held annually along the West Coast and in Texas; participants are never at a loss for new spots to throw lures.

Nevertheless, the real mecca for bass fishing is Florida. With its own strain of bass that grows to immense proportions, Florida is blessed with weather warm enough to facilitate rapid growth and reproduction, and fishermen take full advantage of the almost limitless bodies of water. Throughout the area are literally hundreds of fishing camps. The vast majority are, in reality, nothing more than trailer parks and recreational-vehicle campgrounds, but many are blessed with access to some of the most amazing freshwater fishing in the country. However, numerous exceptional facilities do exist, and the central fishing areas are the Orlando area with its many lakes and entertainment facilities, Lake Okeechobee, and the St. Johns River Basin.

Orlando is extraordinary because world-class fishing is not more than a stone's throw from the local airport and Disney World. The area is blessed with many small streams, ponds, and pits that require nothing more than a guide, a few shiners for bait, and a minimum amount of patience. Several lakes in

FLY-FISHING A SMALL STREAM IN PENNSYLVANIA.

the area, including Lake Kissimmee, Istokpoga, Marion, Stick Farm, and others, offer stunning fishing, wildlife, and fishing camps to meet the needs of any budget. Details are available in any of the local bait shops.

A few hours south of Orlando is world-famous Lake Okeechobee. This lake is the quintessential bass and panfishing experience, and a majority of the local population and economy is geared toward the needs of the fisherman. Dozens of small and large fishing camps surround the lake. Fishermen can stay at inexpensive trailer parks in their own recreational vehicles or rent a completely furnished condo with covered boat dock, guides, and full amenities at such resorts as Anglers Marina in

Clewiston, Florida, or any of several other high-end facilities. It is also possible to stay in historic, picturesque camps directly on the lake. Such a place is the Calusa Lodge in Lakeport, Florida, where restaurant walls are covered with fishing memorabilia of years gone by. Anyone staying there would be well advised to order the alligator appetizer with local hot sauce!

Recognized for its productive waters, Lake Okeechobee, which means Big Waters in local Indian vernacular, has been fished heavily since the turn of the century. It is not uncommon for there to be as many as five thousand boats a day on the lake, and the majority of them will have productive days.

The secret of the lake's continued productivity is its thousands of square acres of littoral zones—shallow areas where fish reproduce. Even though hoards of fishermen invade the lake, it is very easy to get quite lost, and each year deaths occur because unsuspecting and naïve fishermen venture into wilderness areas and are unable to find their way back to civilization. Numerous bait and tackle shops, restaurants, marinas, and boat ramps cater to the needs of the fisherman and add to the local flavor.

Another great fishing area is the St. Johns River and Water Basin. As with other Florida fishing areas, numerous camps exist that provide either minimum or high-end amenities for those seeking the big one. Some of the more colorful camps are Porky's, Big Bass World, Bass World Lodge, Anglers' Paradise Lodge, and others.

Certainly the most desirable times to fish Florida waters is in the dead of winter. This is

also spawning time, and female bass expand to tremendous sizes when carrying eggs. Since this is no secret among fishermen, it is necessary to make your reservations early.

Fishing camps in North America are part of the history of our land, and fishing is often the key to relaxation and rejuvenation, as attested by the more than eleven million fishermen in this country alone. Whether it be a shack made by children or a multimillion-dollar facility designed to meet the needs of the most discriminating, fishing camps are a heritage that is shared with the past. The fishing camp is a place to renew friendships and to demonstrate skills in the face of challenges placed before fishermen by the fish they hunt.

There is something almost spiritual about a stay at a fishing camp, something that should not be ignored. The call of the wild and the freedom inherent in fishing camps speaks deeply to us in voices neither audible nor measurable, and yet it is there. The romance of the fishing experience enhances our lives and allows us to return to our daily worlds as new individuals, reminded that we are worthwhile and that we are capable of meeting the challenges placed before us.

AN OLD PHOTOGRAPH OF A CREEL OF TROUT IN MAINE.

A HAPPY FISHERMAN WITH A MONSTER LAKE TROUT CAUGHT IN OHIO'S LAKE WILLOUGHBY.

THE MIGHTY MUSKIE AND THE THOUSAND ISLANDS

It was four in the afternoon one August day of 1995. My wife, Michele, and I had our sixteen-foot bass boat on the mighty waters of the St. Lawrence seaway. We had spent the previous night in a small motel in Alexandria Bay in the far northwestern corner of New York state. In the morning, after purchasing a map of the local waters—an absolute necessity—at one of several area bait shops, we made our way onto the potentially frightening but beautiful waters of the St. Lawrence River.

BUILT IN 1834 ON WOLFE ISLAND, THIS STRUCTURE HAS BEEN USED BY FISHERMEN IN THE ST. LAWRENCE RIVER SINCE ITS CONSTRUCTION.

IN THIS BREAKFAST ROOM AT A MAINE FISHERMEN'S CAMP, RUSTIC FURNITURE AND A COLLECTION OF DECORATIVE ANTIQUE CANOE PADDLES ADD TO THE MORNING SETTING.

Cruising the waters for close to an hour, we marveled at the vastness and complexities of the area. Michele and I learned quickly to stay out of the way of the oceangoing cargo boats. These behemoths are like floating mountains, and if they don't crush small fishing boats like an elephant crushing a mosquito, then their wake waters will surely swamp small craft. Best to stay out of their way altogether.

Michele and I learned this lesson the hard way. We were throwing lures over a weed bed on the edge of a deep channel when all of a sudden the boat began to rock violently. Because fishing has the capacity to totally occupy every sense possessed by humans, I've often completely lost track of the time, the day, the weather conditions, and every other seemingly important element of reality. I had been preoccupied in this manner when the rocking began. Before I knew it, we were thrown from our seats, groping for anything that would support us. Within a second we both turned to see a monster, ten-story cargo ship within a hundred feet of us. Both of us were completely oblivious to the frantic soundings of the ship's horn and other warning signals. It was on that day that we decided to avoid open waters and, instead, fish the calm and secluded areas that were so famous with other fishermen.

Throughout the remainder of the day, however, we did catch an impressive array of big bass, northern pike, and aggressive panfish. Any fisherman would have been proud, but as the day wore on, we reviewed the charts and found a rocky ledge about seventy feet down near an open channel. We rigged up the downriggers and trolled over the rocky area for more than an hour. Our medium-gage bass rods bent violently under the weight of the downriggers, and I wondered if using the twelve-pound test line wasn't pushing our luck.

In the back of my mind were all of the stories I'd ever heard about muskies. According to local legend, muskies hide in the crevices of deep rock beds, and when hungry they rise violently and ambush any unsuspecting passing fish who just happens into their territory. Muskies are not like other fish. They can safely be compared to an ignited Saturn rocket that knows no bounds and pays little attention to the physical realities of gravity. So on this particular day, when one of the rods sprang free from the downrigger, we hoped for the best.

I picked up my rod and held fast as line peeled out like the string of a kite that is climbing toward the heavens. The drag was set tight, and I knew that the fish would soon stop pulling

A NUMBER OF FISHERMEN TAKE ADVANTAGE OF AN EARLY SPRING HATCH OF MAYFLIES ON A SECLUDED MAINE RIVER.

A FISHERMAN MAKES HIS WAY TO FISHING GROUNDS ON RANGELEY LAKE, MAINE.

27

GRANT'S CAMPS ON THE SHORES OF MAINE'S KENNEBEC LAKE. MORE THAN A HUNDRED YEARS OLD, THE CAMP IS THE QUINTESSENTIAL EXPERIENCE FOR FLY FISHERMEN.

SMALL FISHING CAMP ON THE SHORE OF THE KENNEBEC RIVER IN MAINE.

line from the reel. Still, as the moments dragged on, I couldn't help but look with great concern as more and more line disappeared. Shortly, I could see the shiny core of the reel spool and realized that the fish was quickly taking all the line on the reel. Seconds later panic was now in place as no more line was available. The fish had pulled off all one hundred yards of line, and only a weak knot prevented him from freedom.

With fear in my voice, I asked Michele to put the engine in reverse and follow the line. Within a few seconds I had reeled in several yards of line and had reset the drag to a much-stronger pull.

One does not try to muscle a muskie. It's best to let the drag of the reel and the spring of the rod do the work. But I have to admit that reeling in a big fish is like pulling in an

old tire, at least until the fish nears the boat. Then all hell breaks loose. Muskies, like northern pike, have rows and rows of sharp, needle-pointed teeth, and any wise fisherman knows to keep his hands significantly at bay when handling these monsters.

With renewed effort and hate and anger in his heart, the muskie twisted and turned, sending sprays of water in all directions. Violence marked the moment. But all things sooner or later meet their match, and within minutes the fish was floating near the surface alongside the boat. I lifted the fish into the boat by the gill slits, using great effort and care. Once we had him inside the boat, the hooks—thank god—fell immediately from the fish as he thrashed and slashed his way across the bottom of our shallow bass boat.

It was, however, my time to gloat! For most fishermen their first huge muskie was reason to be proud, but my heart sank when I realized that my cameras were back in the truck. Nonetheless, with great pride and a sense of relief, I lowered the fish back into the choppy waters of the St. Lawrence. There would be another day and another fish.

Locals say that the muskie is the most difficult of all the North American fish to catch. A general rule of thumb is that it takes about a thousand hours of fishing to land a good one. None of that, however, compares with the wonderful story of legendary Mrs. Houser. A stately, dignified woman from Long Island, New York, she had fished the St. Lawrence River for decades trying to hook her first muskie. Finally, in her thirty-fifth year of fishing for muskies, she landed a thirty-six-pound beauty that was the pride of her life.

The St. Lawrence Seaway is, without a doubt, one of the primer historic fishing areas in North America. Hundreds of small camps and lodges occupy the banks along the river, and many more small shelters and camps are housed on tiny spits of land that give the Thousand Islands area its name. Further, dozens of restaurants, lodges, taverns, and clubs offer an ambiance of mounted fish on their walls and endless stories of fishing from those who visit the area each year.

One of the great fishing villages in the area is Wolfe Island. Accessible by ferry or boat from Kingston, Ontario, Wolfe Island is home to several historic lodges and restaurants.

ROADSIDE ADVERTISING FOR A MAINE FISHING GUIDE.

31

THE WOODMAN
HOUSE ON WOLFE
ISLAND OFFERS
ANTIQUE
AMBIANCE, FISHING
GUIDES WITH MORE
EXPERIENCE THAN
YOU COULD EVER
IMAGINE, AND SOME
OF THE BEST
MUSKIE FISHING IN
THE COUNTRY.

THE WOODMAN HOUSE

The Woodman House is a historic, early Victorian structure built in 1835. Today, the floors sag a bit in certain areas, the stairs have creaks and groans, but the house is strong, warm, and comfortable. The house is replete with the ghosts of fishermen past. Photographs of smiling patrons with their catches speak of great battles and of decades gone by. The mounts of many great muskies adorn the walls, and the smells of fresh-cooked meals meander through the hallways.

Purchased by the Woodman family in 1919, the facility was turned into a fishing resort in 1923. Bruce Woodman operated the facility for more than sixty years. When the camp first opened, fishermen were charged six dollars a week for room, three delicious meals a day, and fishing with a guide. Today, Bruce's wife, Margaret, who can fascinate just about anyone with her delightful stories—be sure to ask her to tell you the story of her first thirty-eight-pound muskie that she caught in 1956—and his sons continue to provide room, board, and fishing for the many guests who come to their home.

The Woodman House
Box 26
Wolfe Island, Ontario
K0H 2Y0 Canada
(613) 385-2635

THE RECEPTION
ROOM AT THE
WOODMAN INN,
WOLFE ISLAND, ON
THE ST. LAWRENCE
RIVER, WHICH HAS
BEEN OPENED MORE
THAN A HUNDRED
YEARS AND IS HOME
TO MUSKIE AND
NORTHERN-PIKE
FISHERMEN SINCE
BEFORE THE TURN
OF THE CENTURY.
OWNED BY THE
SAME FAMILY FOR
THE PAST SEVENTY-
FIVE YEARS, THE INN
IS FULL OF FISHING
MEMORABILIA.

GRANT'S KENNEBAGO CAMPS OF MAINE

More than a hundred years ago, Ed Grant, renowned guide from Maine, told of the story of the man who kept a pet trout in a barrel. During a dry season the man dipped out a bit of water each day so the trout would learn to live on less and less water. Finally, the trout lived on no water at all and followed the man around on the ground wearing a tiny pair of snowshoes in winter. Unfortunately one day the trout fell into brook water and drowned!

Ed Grant, well known as a character and storyteller, was the first Maine guide to advertise the wilds and recreational potential of the Maine North Woods. Today, more than a hundred years later, Grant's Kennebago Camps are renowned for their hospitality, beauty, and fishing.

Kennebago Lake, about six hours north of Boston, boasts some of the finest scenery and trout fishing in New England. The lake is crystal clear, and giant trout can be seen twenty feet deep in the water. Moose appear to be everywhere, and loons call their eerie cries throughout the day and night.

CABINS AT GRANT'S CAMP IN MAINE. ESTABLISHED AT THE TURN OF THE CENTURY, THE CAMP IS A HAVEN FOR SERIOUS FLY FISHERMEN. REMEMBER, DON'T FEED THE MOOSE THAT WANDER AROUND THE CAMP AT ALL HOURS OF THE DAY.

A COLLECTION OF
HIGH-END ANTIQUE
CREELS FOUND IN
A FISHERMAN'S
BEDROOM IN
MAINE.

TROUT POND

Fly-fishing only is allowed in the lake, and anglers use historic Rangely Lakes Guide Boats for their fishing excursions. Guests stay in comfortable cabins and eat three hearty meals a day in the dining hall. They should be prepared to drive several miles down a long dirt road, looking out for the moose. On the day of my visit, I counted thirteen in the half-hour drive from the nearby town of Rangely. In the middle of the day, when the fishing slows down, be sure to spend some time with the camp manager, Ralph Wheeler. He's one of the best flytiers in the state, and I'm sure he'll show you his latest designs for nymphs and other regional delicacies.

Grant's Kennebago Camps
P.O. Box 786
Rangely, Maine 04970
(207) 864-3608 (summer)
(207) 282-5264 (winter)

THE CABINS AT GRANT'S CAMP ON KENNEBAGO LAKE IN MAINE, LIKE THE CAMP ITSELF, ARE FULL OF RUSTIC FURNISHINGS AND MORE THAN A CENTURY OF MEMORIES. THE CAMP OFFERS HIGH-QUALITY TROUT FISHING AND AUTHENTIC RUSTIC AMBIANCE.

THE ADIRONDACKS

The Adirondack region of upstate New York was first explored and settled in the early 1830s. The beauty, ruggedness, and natural resources of the area were a dream for those who sought retreat from the difficulties of the city and the Industrial Revolution. In turn-of-the-century publications, the area was described as having crystal-clear lakes, clean air, and a moose behind every tree.

THIS COLLECTION OF OVER TWO HUNDRED ANTIQUE ADIRONDACK GUIDE BOATS IS FROM A PRIVATE FISHING CAMP IN THE ADIRONDACKS.

THE ADIRONDACKS REGION IS RIFE WITH FISHING CAMPS SURE TO PLEASE ANY SPORTSMAN OR FAMILY.

FRICK
FREIDIN
CARPENTER
DUSINBERRE
Peters
HIAWATHA ISLAND

CERTAINLY ONE OF
THE FINEST
FISHING CAMPS IN
AMERICA, THE
LAKE PLACID
LODGE,
CONSTRUCTED IN
1882, IS A WORLD-
CLASS FACILITY
DECORATED IN THE
TRADITIONAL
ADIRONDACK
STYLE.

A PRIVATE BOAT LAUNCH FOR
ADIRONDACK GUIDE BOATS IN UPSTATE
NEW YORK. THE CLUB OWNS SEVERAL
THOUSAND ACRES OF LAND AND WATER
AND HOMES THAT ARE LOCATED DEEP IN
THE WOODS. THE ONLY TRANSPORTATION
TO AND FROM THE HOMES THAT SIT ON
THE SHORES OF SEVERAL INCREDIBLE
TROUT LAKES IS VIA ANTIQUE
ADIRONDACK GUIDE BOATS.

Beginning in the 1870s, wealthy capitalists purchased vast tracts of land and created a distinct style of architecture that came to be known as Adirondack. They built huge structures of logs and timber, retreats that housed the rich and famous for weeks on end. The two activities most commonly engaged in were hunting and fishing, and, in time, many of these same retreats were sold to groups of individuals who made them into private clubs. As time passed, more individuals became involved, and soon, dozens of fishing camps dotted the shores of hundreds of lakes within the six million acres of the Adirondack Park.

Many fishing camps eventually evolved, including private clubs such as the Flyfishing Club of New York, established around the turn of the century, and the New York City Women's Flyfishing Club, which began in 1932.

Located at the southern end of the Adirondack Park about an hour north of Albany is the queen of American lakes, Lake George. The lake is a fisherman's dream. Lake trout and salmon are easily caught, as are northern pike. Panfish seem to jump into the boat one right after the other, and large- and smallmouth bass are there for the fisherman willing to take the time to master the techniques. Bass tournaments are held annually on the lake.

The water of Lake George is sparkling, and mountains and conservation land surround much of this thirty-five-mile-long lake. The southern part of the lake is the home of Lake George Village and a few other towns, such as Bolton Landing and Ticonderoga, which occupy small tracts of shoreline on the north and west sides of the lake. One of the compelling aspects of the lake is the local architecture. Many of the homes surrounding the lake are huge structures completed at the turn of the century in the classical Adirondack style, making boat tours of the

lake both pleasant and fashionable. Dozens of antique mahogany boats are still operating on the lake, and Wednesdays are set aside for sailboat races at the local yacht club. At lunchtime, visitors may wish to visit either the Algonquin Restaurant or the Boat House. Both facilities are directly on the water, and valet parking is available for boats. Additionally, several marinas service the lake. Swimming sites, for those so inclined, are

A BOATHOUSE OF AN ADIRONDACK FLY FISHERMAN.

A FISHERMAN'S BOATHOUSE ON LAKE GEORGE, NEW YORK.

provided at several public beaches. Bait and fishing tackle are available at either Anne's Bait Shop in Bolton Landing or The Outdoorsman Sport Shop in Diamond Point. The owners of both places are loquacious individuals who will reveal all the fishing hot spots as well as discuss the nuances of the latest tackle.

Lake George remains a wild body of water. If one tires of other boats, it is a short ride to secluded areas. Lake George is a deep lake often descending to more than three hundred feet. Numerous small islands with rocky shores dot the lake, and shallow areas are common in the middle of the lake, so it is important to watch depth gages when traveling at high speeds.

THE FISHERMAN'S
CHAPEL ON THE
SHORES OF LAKE
GEORGE, NEW
YORK, THE QUEEN
OF AMERICAN
LAKES.

THIS ADIRONDACK
LEAN-TO SERVES
AS A SHELTER FOR
FISHERMEN AND
OUTDOOR
ENTHUSIASTS ON
RAINY DAYS.

45

THE MAIN LODGE AT THE ALPINE VILLAGE ON THE SHORES OF PICTURESQUE LAKE GEORGE, NEW YORK.

THE CAMPS

ALPINE VILLAGE

Built in 1937, the Alpine Village was constructed by a Swiss-German in the style one might see in the Swiss Alps. Originally filled with handcrafted furniture, the main structure offers comfort and relaxation to guests who come from every state in the Union to enjoy Lake George and the surrounding area. Nuclear engineer Ernie Ippisch purchased the facility in 1986 after tiring of corporate life. With continual improvements, the village became a rustic gem. The main lodge houses a large dining room, a sitting area with huge fireplace, and several rooms with kitchenettes.

Alongside the main lodge are many small log cabins, each picturesque in its own way. The Alpine Village offers docking for a substantial number of boats and a private beach. Individuals may bring their own boats or rent one from any of several marinas that operate in the immediate area. Available are professional fishing guides who can take interested parties out for monster trout and salmon, usually caught by trolling with downriggers. Also available are good guides for exceptional large- and smallmouth bass fishing. In the springtime, largemouths will hit on anything, and it is not uncommon to catch fifty a day. As the year progresses, the smallmouths, found near rock piles and the rocky shoreline,

THE SITTING ROOM
AND FIREPLACE
AREA OF THE
ALPINE VILLAGE
LODGE, A
HANDCRAFTED
VILLAGE THAT
OFFERS SEVERAL
SMALL LOG CABINS
AS WELL AS ROOMS
IN THE MAIN
LODGE.

hit fast and furious on live crawfish. In the winter, ice fishermen pull out huge northern pike and an occasional lake trout.

The Alpine Village is not only a fishing camp but a family vacation resort as well. Prices for rooms range from $59 a night off season to $945 a week for a three-bedroom log cabin that sleeps six. The food in the restaurant is excellent and not overpriced. The Rustic Inn in nearby Lake Luzerne is among the best of the local night spots. It's a great old log cabin, and the owners are full of stories about the Adirondacks. Bartenders Bea and Michele will provide information on some of the local attractions. A rodeo, just down the road, is open Wednesday, Friday, and Saturday nights.

Alpine Village
Box 672
Lake George, New York 12845
(518) 668-2193

TROUT HOUSE VILLAGE RESORT

Farther north in the town of Hague, located on the west side of Lake George, is the Trout House Village Resort. The main house, constructed in 1925, offers nine bedrooms, a library, and dining room for guests. The Village, run by the Patchett family since 1971, includes several log cabins that contain full kitchenettes, bedrooms, fireplaces, and jet tubs.

Along with traditional facilities, the Trout House Village offers a private four-hundred-foot beach, a putting green, canoes, kayaks, and rowboats. Frequently used as a full-service family compound, the facility offers many family-oriented activities. Full-service marinas are located nearby and the Village offers plenty of dock space for those bringing their own boats. The Trout House is the site of the annual June New York Bass Federation fishing tournament where more than two hundred

TROUT HOUSE
VILLAGE IN THE
TOWN OF HAGUE,
NEW YORK, WHICH
SITS ON THE
SHORES OF
PRISTINE LAKE
GEORGE, IS THE
SITE OF NUMEROUS
REGIONAL FISHING
TOURNAMENTS.

THE PATCHETT FAMILY

Trout House Village
PRESENTS
THE LODGE
& CHALET LOG CABINS

WELCOME COME IN

FIREPLACES

fishermen compete for standings and prizes. For an evening out on the town, north a few miles on Route Nine is the Indian Kettle Restaurant. The restaurant, full of rustic furniture, fireplaces, and great ambiance, offers a stunning view of Lake George and has delicious food.

Trout House Village Resort
Hague, New York 12836
(518) 543-6088

LAKE PLACID LODGE

Farther north in the Adirondacks is the town of Lake Placid. The sight of two former winter Olympic games, Lake Placid boasts two world-class ski jumps, a major ski resort, a world-class hockey and ice arena, and a town that rivals any ski area in the world. Quaint and picturesque, the town offers numerous outdoor sports shops, restaurants, glorious lakes, and several stunning resorts. The town backs up to beautiful Mirror Lake with its picturesque beach. The lake is also the site of winter dogsled races.

A few miles outside of town on the shores of pristine Lake Placid, a German family con-structed a classical Adirondack-style home overlooking Whiteface Mountain. The home, built with tall stone fireplaces and huge twig-framed porches was completed in 1882. Eventually, the camp became an inn and opened its doors to the public in 1946. The inn was recently purchased and completely renovated. The facility has now been operating as a full-service lodge that offers not only unbelievable peace and beauty but some of the best golf, tennis, and trout fishing in the North.

The Lake Placid Lodge, as it is known today, is a world-class facility. Meals are served in the dining room and are strictly gourmet,

BUILT IN 1882, THE LAKE PLACID LODGE OFFERS CLASSICAL ADIRONDACK STYLE WITH SOARING FIREPLACES, TWIG AND BIRCH-BARK TRIM THROUGHOUT, AND SUPERB FISHING.

BEDROOM AT THE
LAKE PLACID LODGE
OFFERS UNIQUE
COMFORT AND HIGH
STYLE.

A VIEW OF THE
LOUNGE AREA AT
THE LAKE PLACID
LODGE, WHICH IS
FULL OF ANTIQUE
FISHING
MEMORABILIA. THE
TAVERN ALSO
OFFERS AN
EXCELLENT VIEW
OF WHITE FACE
MOUNTAIN IN THE
ADIRONDACKS.

or visitors may wish to hang out in the bar, which is decorated with antique fishing gear, old photos of the fishing experience, taxidermy, old skis, and related rustic decor of all kinds. Many of the rooms have their own fireplaces and are furnished with classical Adirondack bark furniture. The porches and railings are trimmed with birch and cedar logs, and the view from any of the porches is beyond imagination. The staff at the Lake Placid Lodge are extraordinarily friendly and professional, especially bartender Forest Dewdrop, who loves to tell stories from some of the local folklore. The Lake Placid Lodge not only offers numerous activities but the majority of guests just relax in the lounge or in any of the other comfortable rooms. Rest assured that you will not be disappointed in your visit.

Just a few steps out the back door is historic Lake Placid, with its pristine waters and rugged ambiance of soaring trees and dark, mysterious coves. In these waters are some of the largest rainbow and lake trout found in the East. Those preferring smallmouth bass should just speak up and cast deep-diving crank baits around any of the rocky formations that outline the lake. Guides are often engaged to provide boats and equipment, or visitors can bring their own. If they want to fish something other than the lake, several higher-class streams are nearby. Calling early for reservations is crucial since there is no finer place in the Adirondacks to spend the weekend.

Lake Placid Lodge
Whiteface Inn Road
P.O. Box 550
Lake Placid, New York 12946
(518) 523-2700

BOATHOUSE DOCKS LOCATED AT A PRIVATE TROUT-FISHING FACILITY IN THE ADIRONDACKS.

THE DELAWARE

Certainly one of the greatest trout-fishing rivers in North America is the Delaware watershed. Fueled from the runoffs of the cold waters of the Cannonsville Reservoir, the west branch of the Delaware—just south of Binghamton, New York, and sharing the borders of Pennsylvania and New York—has consistently been called the best tailwater fishery in the East. Abundant with wildlife, including turkey, deer, and bear, the area boasts scenery that is remarkable, unspoiled, and easily accessible. Located just a few hours' drive from New York City, Philadelphia, or Albany, the Delaware and surrounding trout waters are a trout fisherman's paradise.

VIEW OF THE MAIN LODGE, OFFICE, AND TACKLE SHOP AT THE WEST BRANCH ANGLERS RESORT ALONG THE DELAWARE RIVER IN DEPOSIT, NEW YORK.

MASTER FLY-FISHING INSTRUCTOR AND GUIDE JUDD WEISBERG WITH A BEAUTIFUL NINETEEN-INCH BROWN TROUT CAUGHT IN THE WEST BRANCH OF THE DELAWARE RIVER.

The area has been used by serious fly fishermen for hundreds of years, and numerous fly-fishing camps, resorts, fly shops, and guide services exist today to service the needs of the fishing community. Fly-fishing today is a serious endeavor, and those who are serious about trout fishing have carried the sport well into the realm of science and art. To the average individual, one's mind can easily become boggled by the intricacy and complexity of the sport. Having spent time with several devoted trout fishermen over the years, I have often marveled at their level of understanding of the environment that extends well beyond the water where the trout reside. Trout fishermen have often driven me nearly nuts by being able to understand and identify dozens of hatching insects.

Certainly one of the most complex fish on the planet, trout are incredibly picky, and trout fishermen seem to comprehend the constant and subtle changes within the trout's environment. A visit to any good fly-fishing shop will prove my point. There are literally hundreds of different flies, and it seems that all fly fishermen can identify each of them.

Also, a person might be tempted to discuss an analogy between fly and bass fishermen. The two groups are, in reality, worlds apart. Most bass fishermen are high-energy individuals who will move to a new area within two minutes if the fish aren't biting. Fly fishermen, on the other hand, look upon the dilemma as a challenge and will meticulously change flies, which are so subtle in their differences that the average person might not be able to discern any difference whatsoever. Because of the difficulty that bass fishermen often have sitting still, they have occasionally compared fly fishermen to molasses in winter. Some might also suggest that the tastes of fly fishermen are more sophisticated and highbrow than those of the bass fishermen. In reality, to try to compare the personalities and differences between the two distinct groups undoubtedly would prove risky.

Recently, I had the opportunity to fish with fly-fishing guide Judd Weissberg of Lexington, New York. Judd is one of the notoriously exceptional guides I have had the opportunity to get to know over the years. Not only is he a great teacher but he also makes some of the best rustic furniture in the country. Judd works by himself and also guides for the West Branch Anglers and Sportsmen Resort in Deposit, New York.

On the day we fished, it was cold and damp, and we were the only ones on the water. Judd pointed out several variations of hatchings that were occurring and spoke with a great understanding of the need to comprehend the life of the fish we were seeking. On this particular morning we were using a local favorite fly called a patriot because of its red, white, and blue colors. We talked about correct knots and trailer flies, about the subtleties of rods and the intricacies between dry and wet flies. We spoke of the early Hendrickson hatch, the mayflies, and the Eastern Green Drake and the diminutive Trico. On his third cast he landed, with great precision and care, a gorgeous twenty-inch brown trout.

A true fisherman has a profound respect for life. It is uncompromising and unmistakable. As Judd brought the fish to shore, he gently removed the hook and delicately handled his catch to ensure its safety and well-being. Keeping the fish in the water, he carefully lifted it and kept it out of the water only long enough for me to take a quick photograph. After a few moments of revival he released it back to its home and, without a doubt, held the fish in great reverence. As I watched Judd fish, I became aware that the entire process of fishing for this fish was elevated to the realm of the artistic. It was an act of great respect and concern. It was art and humanity at its finest, and a happy reminder of the human capacity for respect of our fellow living creatures.

On that day, we traveled many miles, looking at different sites on the water and visiting different fishing camps. Near the town of Hancock, New York, just a mile or so downstream from Junction Pool, we visited the Wild Rainbow Lodge. Owned by the West Branch Anglers Resort, the Lodge is a picturesque log structure sitting on the shores of the Delaware. As we watched the water, good-looking, massive trout—big enough, so they say, "to wear saddles"—rose in the waters to not only feed but to show off their abilities as great hunters. Nearby, we noticed a pair of gigantic white mute swans. The pair were in courtship display and later approached us, seemingly to show off their beauty as well as their strength. Nesting swans are fiercely territorial, and they made it a point to remind us that this part of the river was theirs.

GUIDE JUDD WEISBERG OFFERS A FEW CASTING TIPS TO MICHELE KYLLOE AS SHE PRACTICES ON THE WELL-STOCKED POND OF THE WEST BRANCH ANGLERS RESORT.

THE CAMPS

An abundance of camps, fly shops, guide services, and resorts exist in this area. Certainly one of the best is the West Branch Anglers and Sportsmen's Resort in Deposit, New York. On the banks of the Delaware, the resort is the quintessential experience for the fly fisherman. The main resort offers fifteen or so small- to medium-size log cabins for rent that are modern, clean, exceptionally well-maintained, and comfortable. They also have a well-stocked fly shop that offers more variations on a theme than the world has insects. The beauty of the facility is that, by being housed on the stream, they can and are aware of the subtleties in the hatching on the water just outside their doorsteps.

West Branch guides are top-notch, calm, gentle people, who excel at teaching and offer a reverence for the sport that is apparent and uncommon. The individuals who work the fly shop are seasoned pros themselves and can pick out the differences in insects and flies with remarkable clarity. The resort also offers a fully stocked pond where fishermen can perfect their techniques under the expert tutelage of their instructors. Or they can rent a boat

and float sections of the river that may be hard to get to without one.

The resort also offers an exceptional school for fly-fishing. Its programs cover the intricacies of equipment, casting, presentation, bug identification, behavior, flytying, and more. They offer programs of varying lengths for all levels of expertise as well as programs for women, apprentices, and advanced flytying.

Those who choose to eat in the West Branch dining hall will find that the cooks will ensure a great meal at just about any time of the day, or they can cook their own meals along with other guests in a pavilion-style area and enjoy the company of others who have similar interests.

For visitors so interested, the lodge staff will also provide trips to other important rivers in the area, including the Beaverkill, Willowemoc, the East Branch, or the Main Delaware. Each of these rivers offers its own special subtleties and uniqueness.

The West Branch also owns the secluded Wild Rainbow Lodge. Corporations and small groups often prefer private sites, and the Rainbow Lodge is perfect for retreats. The muted swans, as mentioned earlier, are located just out the back door, and almost any time of

A SIGN FOR A TROUT-FISHING RESORT IN UPSTATE NEW YORK.

A SIGN FOR A TROUT-FISHING RESORT IN UPSTATE NEW YORK.

the day wild turkeys wander up to the game feeder for a free meal, offering their antics to guests, who find them quite entertaining. Often squirrels visit with the turkeys, and one big tom enjoys tackling them, holding them down with one foot while he continues to feed, and then releasing them when he feels like it. This game goes on for quite some time and is usually enough of an entertaining distraction to delay most fishing.

I have always felt that anyone can build a resort, but few people are capable of managing it. The people at West Branch are open, friendly individuals who love what they do for a living and love sharing their passions with others. This is one place that won't disappoint.

West Branch Anglers and
Sportsmen's Resort
150 Faulkner Road
P.O. Box 102
Deposit, New York 13754
(607) 467-5525
(607) 467-2215 (fax)

INDIVIDUAL CABINS AT THE WEST BRANCH ANGLERS RESORT LINE THE SHORES OF THE DELAWARE RIVER.

THE NORTHERN PIKE

Northern pike are the cruise missiles of fresh waters. They will swim long distances at incredible speeds to make a kill. I have seen them in very clear waters streak like meteors and slam into prey with incredible violence. They have sawlike pointed teeth that are capable of holding prey and puncturing organs for a quick death. Smart fishermen know to keep their hands away from the pikes' mouths.

A STRINGER OF
NORTHERN PIKE
FROM A FISHING
EXCURSION IN
MICHIGAN.

GUIDE JOHN ORAVEC
OF WATERPORT, NEW
YORK, RELEASING
ANOTHER MONSTER
FISH CAUGHT ON THE
ST. LAWRENCE RIVER.

Early ice-fishing catches and my first really big northern were caught while fishing the Boundary Waters Canoe Area just north of Ely, Minnesota. I was with wildlife cinematographer Neil Rettig and a few others for a week of fishing and canoeing in the far northern lakes of the district. We had paddled in for two days and had begun fishing on the morning of the third day.

The black flies throughout the trip were unbelievable. They are truly the guardians of the wilderness as they are capable of causing terror in everyone caught in an attack. A few days before our visit, a local bait-shop owner mentioned his dog had to be shot because it had been tied to a tree, and the black flies had infested its nose, ears, and eyes, driving the poor dog howling mad.

The flies were always present on the tiny island where we set up camp, but dinner times were the most brutal. Thousands of these kamikazes would swarm anyone who stood still for even a few seconds. The bite of a black fly causes a sharp, stinging sensation and near-hysterical itching. A few days later, red welts show up and don't leave for a week. A Native American guide I once hired wore sprigs of cedar behind his ears as a repellent. In theory it's a great idea. Cedar contains natural insect repellents, but it brought me little relief from the nasty creatures.

Despite the flies, Neil and I were fishing from a small canoe using large Mepps lures and having good success around fallen trees, rocks, and other obstructions. We caught a number of aggressive smallmouth bass as well as several two- and three-foot-long northerns. We were using light gear, and we both realized that sooner or later our lines would snap under the weight of a large fish.

About midday, we entered a small cove lined with rocks and fallen trees. The water was quite shallow and crystal clear. I was in the bow and cast a lure across a sandy shallow area toward a large rock overhang. As the lure struck the water, I noticed a swirl of water twenty yards away. A monster pike had broken cover and was bearing down on my lure like a torpedo. Straight and true he went. There was no doubt about his intentions. I cranked the lure at a steady pace, and within a few seconds his alligator jaws engulfed the lure. I set the hook lightly; realizing that I had light tackle, I wanted as little stress on the fish and tackle as possible. The line held and pulled tight as the fish rolled and exposed his yellow belly. I knew that the drag on my reel was set too tight when no line peeled off. The pole bent furiously as I watched the fish charge directly off the bow of the boat. It was a calm day, and the water was perfectly still. Within a few moments, the canoe began moving toward deeper waters, slowly at first and then we picked up steam. The fish was so large, it was towing the canoe with two people in it across the lake. In time, the fish tired, and I was able to turn him after several minutes. Shortly, we had him near the side of the boat. His size was incredible, easily the largest pike I had ever seen in photographs or real life.

As the fish gave in to my efforts, he lay on his side alongside of the boat. The lure was precariously caught in a small piece of tissue on the corner of his mouth. If he had taken the lure into his mouth, he easily could have cut the line as we were not using wire leaders. My intentions were to pull in as much line as possible and grab him in his gill slits since the large net we had would have been useless on a fish that size. As we got closer to him, we both realized that this was a monster fish, one that was due great respect. He was much larger than one could imagine and was no doubt capable of great feats of strength. As I

admired him, he worked his jaws for air and seemed almost repulsed by the indignity of being forced on his side by mere humans. With a roll of his eyes and lunge of his tail that exploded the water, he swam away with no apparent concern. My line finally gave in to his great strength, and within a few minutes the fish disappeared into the depths of the lake, never to be seen by me again.

He would bear the scars of his contact with humans until the hook rusted and settled to the bottom of crystal-clear waters. He was an honorable fish, and I take delight in knowing that I had contact with him if only for a few seconds. This was his world, and he was the master. I felt humbled by a creature so powerful and strong that any freshwater creatures, including ducks and muskrats, would have been terrified of his presence. My only

hope is that he had many offspring.

From that day on, I have been leery of putting my feet in waters where northerns and muskies exist. If one were to grab onto a foot, they could do severe damage and make life miserable for quite some time. They are, in reality, miniature alligators with hundreds of needle-sharp teeth, and the large ones rule their waters with strong jaws and mean temperaments.

Equally important is the fact that they are courageous. On many occasions I have caught northern pike that were only a few inches long. The lures that they attacked were bigger than the fish. On other occasions, we have caught them with fish in their stomachs that were almost as large as the pikes themselves. They are a worthy opponent to those who seek to hunt them.

THE EAST BAY FISHING CAMP IN THE BOUNDARY WATERS CANOE AREA NORTH OF ELY, MINNESOTA, SPECIALIZES IN FISHING FOR NORTHERN PIKE.

THE TANTALIZING TROUT
OF THE ROCKIES

Until the summer of 1983, fly-fishing was a mystery to me. Before then, in all honesty, I found myself too impetuous and anxious for the details necessary to the sport. The few fly fishermen I knew and had spent time with almost ruined the sport for me. I watched them spend hours fishing one spot, and if, after several minutes, they didn't catch anything, they carefully and meticulously changed the flies and started casting all over again. This would go on for hours. For the life of me, I could never understand how the changing of a fly, especially one so similar to the original, could possibly entice fish to hit, even after fishing the same pool for hours on end.

MICHELE KYLLOE
DISPLAYS A TWENTY-
TWO-INCH WYOMING
BROWN TROUT
CAUGHT ON SPINNING
GEAR IN THE GREEN
RIVER.

GUIDE KEITH SHORT
CASTING IN THE GREEN
RIVER EAST OF
JACKSON, WYOMING.

A FLY FISHERMAN TRIES HIS LUCK WITH A FEW EARLY-SPRINGTIME CASTS.

Fly-fishing has often been perceived by the common man (such as myself) as an erudite and sometimes pompous activity, one where stuffy, high-brow men could wear expensive outfits, travel to exotic places, and act impressed and overjoyed when they caught an eight-inch fish. Big deal! Give me a good bass rod, a small boat, and a weed-bed lake, and I'll show anyone what fishing should be. I used to believe that as an educated man I must show tolerance for those less fortunate in their understanding than I. Let the often-pretentious and uninformed lovers of fly-fishing be; they were harmless anyway. If they wanted to spend their bountiful dollars on equipment, the sometimes-ostentatious raiment, and expensive travel, let them. Their expenditures were good for the economy.

My attitude changed in the summer of 1983, the year my friends Harry Salmen and Ann Murphy of Tucson, Arizona, invited me for a week of fishing in an obscure Rocky Mountain valley. Located in the central to southern part of Colorado, the area was surrounded by snow-capped, towering peaks. Off in the distance, real cowboys daily checked their herds. One afternoon they thrilled us by riding into our camp to check us out. Occasionally, a mountain lioness and her two cubs made themselves visible as they roamed the valley below us, and above us a badger warily watched us as he went about his daily business.

The stream that ran by our camp meandered past our tents, seemingly with great wisdom bringing life to the region and peace to our beautiful setting. At its widest point, the stream was no more than fifteen feet across. Often, deep channels cut through the grasslands and narrowed it to a smaller eight-to-ten feet across. It was surrounded with low-lying grass where shorebirds pecked the soft banks. Picturesque and pristine, it was a respite from the hectic life I'd left behind.

To fish the stream, I initially tried a traditional fly-rod approach, and upon returning to camp, I would produce one or two rainbow trout—shimmering, iridescent, and beautiful. My comrades, however, consistently brought in at least four, reporting that they had each released several others.

In time, I realized that stealth was the answer. Nothing was more ominous to fish than the sudden appearance of a dark looming shadow. Fish, after all, are skittish and hypersensitive to changes and vibrations. I actually began crawling upstream on my stomach, and I remained in that position for several casts. Not surprisingly, my strike ratio dramatically increased. But there was a price to pay; my clothes were soaking wet and muddy after a few minutes of this new approach/avoidance posture. To solve the problem, I donned my Goretex wind pants and jacket on my next outing.

A CABIN AT THE CRESCENT H RANCH IN WYOMING, OVERLOOKING TROUT POND WITH SOME OF THE BIGGEST FISH IN THE WEST. NOT ONLY DO THE CAMP HORSES WANDER IN THE FRONT YARD BUT SO DO ELK, DEER, AND AN OCCASIONAL BLACK OR GRIZZLY BEAR.

On the evening bite, I struggled while changing flies and managed to partially hook myself as I fumbled with a variety of tangled flies and leaders. So the following morning, I borrowed a fishing vest that had assorted pockets and compartments with easy access. I also borrowed an extra hat and hung flies from the soft material that made up the brim and realized that my boots needed to be sealed as the cold Rocky Mountain waters seeped slowly through the seams and eventually made my life less than comfortable.

It was on that day that I realized there were more appropriate and specifically designed outfits for my situation. Humbly, at the end of the week, I entered my favorite fishing store and purchased chest-high, waterproof waders, a fly vest, and a hat that today is the semipermanent home for an assortment of flies and hooks. As I wore my new outfit on later fishing forays, I realized that I had joined the elite and erudite fly-fishing

EQUIPMENT ROOM AT THE CRESCENT H RANCH IN WYOMING. THE CAMP SPECIALIZES IN FLY-FISHING THE WYOMING RIVERS AND OFFERS WEEK-LONG PACKAGES FOR BOTH BEGINNERS AND ADVANCED FISHERMEN.

GUIDE KEITH SHORT OF JACKSON, WYOMING, HOLDS A TWENTY-TWO-INCH BROWN TROUT CAUGHT IN THE GREEN RIVER, WYOMING.

community of the world. I was thankful that those who came before me had thought of fishing necessities that would make my life significantly more comfortable. I now offer my profound apologies to those whom I had long regarded as toplofty and pompous. I am now one of them.

My week of fishing in the Rockies was not without its moment of doubt and faith. One morning as I clandestinely approached a section of narrows on the stream, I managed to crawl within a few inches of a relaxing rattlesnake.

This, I was acutely aware, was a dangerous situation. All I could do was freeze. I felt my heartbeat rise like the mountains that surrounded me, and I realized that if I got bitten, help was several hours away. Within a few sec-

onds, the snake coiled, becoming agitated, and he pulled his head back from mine, ready to strike. The mere memory still makes my blood pressure rise.

Seconds later, the snake sprang at my face. I slammed my head into the mud, and it grabbed firmly onto my hat. I rolled away and ran several yards before I turned to see the rattler twisting with my hat firmly in its jaws. It was not a pleasant sight. Eventually, the snake released his grip and made his way to a nearby rock pile.

Later that evening, I laughed at the situation with my friends around the campfire. During the next few days I changed my approach to include significantly more noise and to avoid obvious rock piles. To this day, I swear that the most important piece of fishing

FISHING FOR BROWN AND RAINBOW TROUT ALONG THE GREEN RIVER IN WYOMING.

equipment is a good hat.

It was also during this trip that I first marveled at the beauty of rainbow trout. Exceptionally well balanced, the fish are an artist's dream. Their subtle colors blend into each other as finely as an impressionist's landscape. The rainbow's tenacity to survive in almost inhospitable waters is remarkable in and of itself. And, God, they taste great.

This magnificent week ended, unfortunately, with a serious mishap. My accident-prone friend Harry Salmen was walking across a small log and fell sideways into a stream. On his way down, he hit a jagged branch and opened a hole in his leg deep enough to expose his femur. We had to carry him out of the mountains for more than two miles uphill to our vehicles and then drive three hours to the nearest health center. I don't know what caused me more stress—Harry's accident or my encounter with the rattlesnake. But despite the misfortune, I love fly-fishing!

JACKSON HOLE

Mecca for the millions of trout lovers is Jackson, Wyoming. I have fished there many times over the years, and the Snake River and surrounding waters, as well as the Grand Tetons, are both stunning and awe-inspiring. I usually spend a week or more fishing the waters of Yellowstone Park and the surrounding areas every year. After a few days, we wander south and spend time in the New Fork, Green, and Snake Rivers.

My first encounter with the area was several years ago. We hired a guide (a necessity for any area one has never fished) and floated down the Snake River just outside of Jackson. Since it was early spring, several animals had frequented the area, and we were quite surprised as a full-grown bull moose sauntered quietly within ten yards of us. He took a deep drink, stared at us for a few moments, and then wandered to the other side of the river.

On our first Jackson fishing trip, it soon

A BAIT SHOP IN JACKSON, WYOMING.

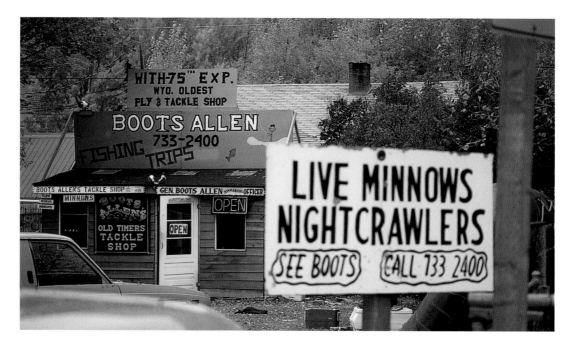

became apparent that the local cutthroat trout were both plentiful and serious fighters. Though many choose to fish the river with fly rods, we chose to use spinning gear. We pulled one right after the other into the boat. I was a bit surprised that it was necessary to cast right into the fastest-moving waters. At first, I thought the eddies and calm waters would be productive, but the big ones were right in the white water, and when they hit, it was like gangbusters.

This was the first time that I had seen so many fish dance on the water—not just once or twice, but several jumps for each fish as they soared high above the water. On that day, we caught probably fifty cutthroat trout, and we decided to plan our next vacation to coin-cide with peak Grand Teton fishing.

In 1995, we met one of the best guides we ever hired. Keith Shorts had fished the waters of the Grand Tetons for many years, and he demonstrated an intimate knowledge of the Wind River Range. We asked several people for the name of a few exceptional guides, and Keith's name came up repeatedly. Naturally, we called him and mentioned that we would like to find a remote spot away from the town and other fishermen. On a Friday in early October, Keith met us at our hotel room way before dawn. We exchanged greetings and shortly departed in two vehicles for the private fishing grounds of a veteran fly-fishing guide.

After an hour-and-a-half drive, we pulled off onto a winding dirt road. Out of necessity,

FULL MEALS, GREAT RUSTIC AMBIANCE, AND PLENTY OF FISHING AWAIT GUESTS OF THE MEADOW CREEK LODGE IN IDAHO WHO ARE WILLING TO TRAVEL TO GET THERE.

we drove slowly to avoid hitting the pronghorn antelope or occasional moose that wandered onto the road. Within a half hour, we were on the shores of the Green River, smiling at each other as we watched the sunrise. After shuttling cars for another forty-five minutes, we boarded the boat that would take us to fisherman's paradise.

I believe that fishing guides in the Rocky Mountains have to work harder than guides from other parts of the country. Since there are no motors on the boats, the guides row their shallow-bottom boats for the entire day's fishing. We knew, however, within the hour that it would be a slow day fishing. On several occasions, Keith mentioned he had caught over 150 fish on this particular section of the Green River. He repeatedly apologized for the slow fishing. We were not disappointed in the least with our catch of more than twenty rainbow and brown trout by the end of the day. All the fish were above twenty inches and a few were above twenty-four inches. Quite frankly, I could not imagine catching a hundred of these fish in one day.

THE CAMPS

I certainly have not seen all the many fishing camps in the Rocky Mountains, but the few where I have spent time are wonderful. I recommend any of the following camps:

CRESCENT H RANCH

Crescent H Ranch was built in 1927 and today stands as one of the greatest fishing camps of the Rocky Mountains. Several small rustic cabins, blended well into the spectacular beauty of the mountains, house residents while in camp. Meals are prepared in the main log lodge, which is full of hunting and fishing trophies, antique elk-antler furniture, giant fireplaces, and more memories than one could experience in a lifetime. The food is abundant and strictly gourmet. Game dishes often include venison, elk, pheasant, and quail.

The ranch occupies more than 1,700 acres of pristine woodlands and mountain scenery. Elk, moose, deer, and an occasional bear wander freely across the lands of Crescent H Ranch. Eagles and other birds of prey are a daily sight from the porches of the lodge or cabins.

The Crescent H fishing, as with other lodges in the area, is extraordinary. Crescent H, however, has more than seven miles of private streams on the property, and the Snake and Yellowstone Rivers are just a short hop down the road. The ranch also has a fully stocked Orvis store on the grounds. The guides for the ranch are strictly professional. A favorite of many guests is the one-week fly-fishing school. One guide is assigned to two individuals. By the end of the week, guests will have experienced some of the greatest fishing and instruction in the land, acquiring enough knowledge for a lifetime of enjoyment.

While at the Crescent H, guests might want to venture out on a guided fishing trip on horseback. Or they can just hang out and enjoy some of the most spectacular scenery anywhere.

Crescent H Ranch
S.C. Rivermeadows
P.O. Box 347
Wilson, Wyoming 83914
(307) 733-3674
(307) 733-8475 (fax)

THE MAIN LODGE OF THE CRESCENT H RANCH, WHICH WAS CONSTRUCTED IN THE 1930S AND OFFERS SPECTACULAR SCENERY, EXTRAORDINARY FISHING, AND RUSTIC AMBIANCE.

PAIR OF
EXTRAORDINARY
ELK-ANTLER ARM
CHAIRS
CONSTRUCTED IN
THE 1930S,
PRESENTLY OWNED
BY THE CRESCENT
H RANCH.

THE FRONT PORCH
OF THE LIARS'
CLUB, A PRIVATE
HIDEOUT AT THE
CRESCENT H
RANCH THAT
DOUBLES AS A
FLY-TYING
FACILITY,
CLASSROOM, AND
EQUIPMENT ROOM.

A SITTING ROOM AT THE SPOTTED HORSE RANCH, LOCATED ON THE SHORES OF THE HOBACK RIVER JUST SOUTH OF JACKSON, WYOMING.

THE SPOTTED HORSE RANCH

The Spotted Horse Ranch is another of the great historic fishing camps of the Rocky Mountains. Located about a half hour south of Jackson, the ranch is situated on the shores of the pristine Hoback River. Individual log guest cabins with full modern conveniences offer visitors the ambiance of the rustic setting and the joys of world-class trout fishing just a few feet from their front doors.

The log dining hall and lounge at the Spotted Horse are full of antique fishing memorabilia and other interesting items reminiscent of the Rocky Mountains. Tired muscles from pulling in "big ones" all day can be soothed in either a sauna or hot tub.

Meals are served family style, and guests are assured of both quality and quantity in the three meals cooked fresh each day. If desired, the chef will cook up the day's catch. Cutthroat, browns, and rainbows are plentiful.

As with other ranches in the area, full-day guided trips are available on the Snake, Hoback, Salt, New Fork, or Green Rivers.

**The Spotted Horse Ranch
Star Route 43
Jackson Hole, Wyoming 83001
(307) 733-2097**

FLY-FISHING FOR
MONSTER TROUT IS
OFTEN DONE RIGHT
OUT THE BACK DOOR
AT THE SPOTTED
HORSE RANCH IN
WYOMING.

THE MAIN LODGE
AT ELK CREEK
RANCH IN ISLAND
PARK, IDAHO,
SERVES MEALS
FAMILY STYLE,
AND IF GUESTS
CAN'T CATCH
THEIR TROUT
LIMITS BY SEVEN
A.M. AT THIS
PLACE, THEY'RE
NOT TRYING.

ELK CREEK RANCH

The Elk Creek Ranch is the epitome of rustic settings. Located in the wilds of Idaho, a few hours west of Yellowstone Park, the ranch is in the heart of Idaho's famous trout country. Bear, moose, and elk are often seen wandering through the beautiful yet wild grounds of the ranch. Log cabin guest cottages, replete with rustic furnishings and fireplaces, offer residents peace and tranquility.

Fishing for huge eastern brook and rainbow trout, many up to five pounds, occurs just outside the main lodge in the ranch's private lake. During my October visit, thousands of migratory ducks were residing on the still waters, and huge trout rose to snatch the remaining insects that mistakenly fell from the sky.

Elk Creek, situated nearby, is another spot known for huge fish, or fishermen tired of the immediate waters can travel a bit to the renowned waters of the Madison, Firehole, Gibbons, and Gallatin Rivers. A little farther out, anglers from all across the country fish the Hebgen and Henry's Lakes as well as the Island Park Reservoir for fish so large that they are commonly referred to as "tackle busters."

Meals are included in the vacation packages, and one never walks away from the dining table wanting for more. In the evenings, guests lounge in front of the fireplace in the log cabin main lodge and relax in antique leather chairs.

Elk Creek Ranch
Box 2
Island Park, Idaho 83429
(208) 558-7404

SECLUDED CABINS AT ELK
CREEK RANCH IN ISLAND PARK,
IDAHO, OFFER A SERIOUS
WILDERNESS EXPERIENCE FOR
THOSE SEEKING SOLITUDE AND
EXTRAORDINARY FLY-FISHING.

ONE OF SEVERAL OUT
CAMPS AT MEADOW
CREEK LODGE IN IDAHO,
WHERE GUESTS FISH
RIGHT OUT THE BACK
DOOR.

81

THE MIGHTY SALMON

I n late summer of 1989, I was invited by my good friend, artist Jack Gunter of Camano Island, Washington, to fish for the mighty king salmon near the Campbell River on Vancouver Island. Jack was part of a group of fifteen individuals who had scheduled a fishing excursion to Painters Lodge in the town of Campbell River about five hours north of Victoria. I was the sixteenth person.

FLY-FISHING THE CAMPBELL RIVER. BLACK BEARS ARE OFTEN SEEN ON THE SHORES, SCROUNGING FOR REMAINS OF FISH CARCASSES AFTER THE SPAWN.

Daybreak on the Campbell River arrived with cold air and steam off the water. At first light, I watched dozens of fishermen line up on the docks and wait for their guides to appear. On signal, those with reservations boarded small Boston Whalers and departed from the docks with little fanfare and hope in their hearts. Each boat contained two fishermen and a guide. Dozens of boats left the mooring. As they cruised across the sound, the fishermen were reminded of the need to wear warm clothing—the sting of cold winds can tug deeply at a person.

Within fifteen minutes of skimming across the water, we arrived at the guide's favorite bait shop, where we ordered three dozen shiners. Once the boats were loaded, we made our way to the bay and joined hundreds of other boats in our quest for the "king."

One of several ways to fish for king salmon is "moochin'." A bamboo or graphite fly rod is used in the traditional trolling method. Every few minutes, however, the boat is reversed, and the sinker and bait are allowed to fall deeper into the ocean. After a few seconds, the boat again moves forward and travels in a line that the guide hopes can produce fish.

For three days we mooched the bays of the Pacific Ocean. My friend Jack caught the first salmon, and during his fight I kindly offered my assistance reeling in the fish. My offer was rejected, and Jack soon was the proud owner of a thirty-five-pound king.

Shortly after the capture of his king, my line pulled tight, and I set the hook like a pro. May not be big, but at least it's a fish, I thought to myself. In short order, I had my fish at the side of the boat, and without much fanfare but with much ribbing from my fishing partner, I cut loose the small sand shark, known commonly as a dogfish, that had attacked my line.

By the end of the day, I had caught at least twenty "doggies," and by the end of the three-day fishing excursion, I was certain I had landed more than fifty of the nasty little creatures. Every person in my group had

A PAIR OF TASTY SALMON CAUGHT WHILE "MOOCHING" THE CAMPBELL RIVER.

landed a king, and most had taken their two-a-day limit. Unfortunately, I caught no salmon, but I had a great time. Jack's friends were all professional people, and our conversations went on for hours after the sun set.

Once we returned to Seattle, I had a few days before I had to fly back to Boston. While driving toward the Olympia Rain Forest, a day's drive from Seattle, I decided to call a friend in Chicago. Michele Keller was at work, and we chatted for several minutes. Though I had not known Michele for long, I gathered my courage and invited her to Seattle for a few days of sight-seeing and a visit to Victoria, the magical city on Vancouver Island. She said that she would think about it, and asked me to call her the next day.

When I called Michele the next day, she said she would be in Seattle the following

A GUIDE ALONG THE
CAMPBELL RIVER
BRINGS HOME THE
MORNING'S CATCH.

for at least a pink salmon. Unfortunately, I was cursed with another and then another dogfish. To this day I hate them.

Then Michele's line went tight and yards of line peeled off the reel. Within seconds, she had picked up the pole and properly set the hook. Our guide, however, being of masculine gender and of the old-school attitudes, grabbed the pole from Michele's hands and handed it to me, shouting that this fish was too big for her. It could only be landed by a man. I will never forget the look on Michele's face as I fought my first king salmon. Her expression was something between rage and disgust.

About fifteen minutes later, I had the fish in the boat and was beaming prouder than any man could. It was that day I decided to marry

morning, and she was looking forward to a few days of relaxation. Upon her arrival, we went immediately to Victoria and then back to the Campbell River and to the Campbell River Lodge. When I invited her to the West Coast, I do not believe in her wildest dreams she even considered we would be fishing cold Pacific waters before sunrise.

Nonetheless, at four A.M. the following morning we were on a pier eagerly waiting our Indian guide who was represented as one of the best guides in the business. Within the hour, we had picked up our bait and were moochin' the narrows north of the Campbell River. Almost immediately my line pulled tight, and as I reeled in my catch, I was hoping

TWO NICE KING
SALMON CAUGHT BY
RALPH AND MICHELE
KYLLOE.

Michele. To this day, however, I have to live with the occasional wrath of my wife for the unthinking act of our chauvinistic guide. His inconsiderate treatment of Michele was thoughtless and insensitive. Nonetheless, once in a long while, late in the evenings, and only when I'm alone, I smile to myself and thank the lord that he handed me the rod. God forgive me for my lack of consideration!

After I caught my fish, Michele landed seven good-size "pinkies." And at the end of the fishing day, as we helped clean the salmon we had caught, we noticed two mature bald eagles in a tree directly across from the fish-cleaning station, some one hundred feet away. Our guide mentioned that we should throw the fish heads in their direction. We were pleasantly surprised when the eagles swooped

THE ENTRANCE TO THE CAMPBELL RIVER LODGE.

down and picked up the fish heads off the rocky shore just twenty feet from us.

The chef at the Campbell River Lodge was gracious enough to prepare one of our pinkies for us, and that afternoon we ate fresh-caught salmon with hollandaise sauce, vegetables, and rice, and drank a few bottles of locally brewed beer. We sat overlooking the magnificent Campbell River, watching the eagles as they picked clean the fish remnants we provided for them. It was the most memorable meal I ever had and was made far better by the fact that my first forty-pound king salmon (albeit, stolen from my future wife by an unthinking guide) was safely off to the smokehouse.

New Adventures

The following year, I got a call from my old friend Mike Beecher, who was living just south of Seattle. As younger men, both Michael and I were involved in falconry, and we often flew our birds together in hunt. Michael had, for the past several years, fished the waters off Tofino and Ucluelet on the western shores of Vancouver. We agreed to meet in late August for the autumn bite in the seacoast town of Ucluelet.

In the morning of our first fishing day, the waters were calm inside the harbor. But once outside the protective narrows, the seas were swelling to ten feet. Within the first hour Michele became violently ill, and I was soon no better. Nonetheless, one of the poles tipped dramatically and line began peeling off at an impressive rate. As I grabbed the pole and set the hook, I felt a wave of nausea overwhelm me. All I could do was hang over the side and succumb to the waves of nausea as I reeled in my fish. While this was going on, the boat was thrown violently sideways. I lost my footing and wound up on my back against the bottom of the boat.

Through all this, I managed to land a thirty-pound king salmon. Whenever I think of that day now, I am happy that no one had a video of the experience as, no doubt, it was one of the most ridiculous scenes ever to happen in the realm of fishing.

We survived the week, however, placing medicated patches on ourselves to combat the pall of seasickness. Throughout the week we managed to catch a few fish as we rode the waves that were so capable of creating havoc within our bodies. Near the end of the experience, I longed for some peaceful bass fishing on the calm waters of my home, Lake George, New York.

Nevertheless, I was persistent. On the day of our departure and our planned return to the work world, I stopped the car after driving four hours toward the airport and told Michele that I had not had enough fishing for king salmon. Traveling to Vancouver from upstate New York is expensive, and the thought occurred to me that we may not get back to this place again for quite sometime. Without much discussion, we turned around and headed back to Ucluelet. Once there, we hired guide Ken Rite of Island West Resort, who was willing to take us out for the evening bite. He was a young, cocky individual who seemed to know what he was doing, so we signed on and agreed to leave within the hour.

Michele and I both placed patches on our necks and prepared ourselves for the evening's adventure. Shortly, we were out of the bay and competing for a point of rock with dozens of other boats. The waves crashed spectacularly on the rocky shoreline as we maneuvered the

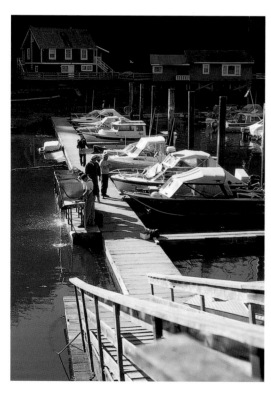

Salmon-fishing boats in the town of Ucluelet, British Vancouver Island.

FIGHTING A BIG KING SALMON OFF THE SHORES
OF TOFFINO, BRITISH COLUMBIA.

IT'S MAN AGAINST SALMON ALONG THE COAST
OF UCLUELET, VANCOUVER ISLAND.

boat within twenty feet of land. As we crossed the point, the first pole violently jerked aft and began peeling out line like gangbusters. The captain sounded the horn as the first salmon broke surface and leaped like a ballerina in the air. The waves were now crashing against the bow of the boat, and the captain had to bring the boat sharply to port to avoid the menacing rocks that were now only a few feet from us.

In seconds, we were a safe distance from the shore and the captain raced to raise the downriggers to avoid tangling my line. Luck was not with us, however, because by the time the first downrigger was at surface, my monster salmon had passed over the second downrigger cable and had broken the line that would have sealed his fate. I was devastated, and the guide knew it.

"Here, take this one," he shouted to me as another fish had taken the second line just moments after the first hook-up. The guide redeemed himself. I landed a forty-pounder about ten minutes later and felt a glow of warmth and a rush of strength course through my body. Moments later another line tightened and then another. This time both Michele and I had huge fish on line. Her fish swung hard to port and mine raced directly off the stern. Both surfaced suddenly and danced in the air. Within a few minutes, we had both fish on board, and the guide had both lines back in the water as Michele maneuvered the boat to the magical spot just off the point of rocks.

Within two minutes, both lines tightened again and we fought a laudable battle against mighty warriors who were being ripped from their elements and were not about to give up their lives without an all-out effort.

Salmon are marvelously deceptive fish. Often they will surface and swim right at fishermen without their knowledge. A fisherman

might feel the line go limp, and he relaxes. Just then, the salmon breaks water and spits the hook laughingly in the fisherman's face. Salmon do not give up; even once in the boat they fight so much that they have to be clubbed into unconsciousness to keep them from breaking equipment and the bones of their hunters.

This was how I lost my third fish of the day. But Michele still had hers, and the fish now swam violently toward the bow. At that point, it was a necessity for one of us to cross a six-inch-wide walkway, through violent waves and a fighting fish still on line to get to the bow of the boat. I jumped onto the walkway and made my way precariously toward the bow with the rod that Michele had handed me. As I reached the front of the boat a massive wave crashed around the ship. I was suddenly chest

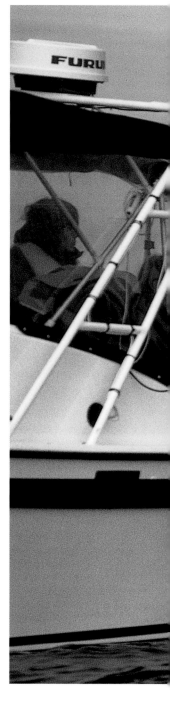

FISHERMAN WITH A FIFTY-POUND HALIBUT OFF THE PACIFIC COAST.

A GUIDE AND A HAPPY
FISHERMAN LANDING A
KING SALMON OFF THE
COAST OF TOFFINO,
BRITISH COLUMBIA.

deep in the Pacific Ocean as water submerged the bow of the boat. I hung on for my life. Moments later the boat resurfaced, and I continued my battle with a fish that was fighting for his life. Fortunately, the line held, and I reeled in my second salmon of the day. At the time, I was not aware of the danger that I was in. Violent seas have taken the lives of many "landlubbers and experienced sailors alike." Michele, the captain, and I promptly put on life vests after the incident.

On that day, in two hours of fishing, and in violent seas, we landed seven forty-pound king salmon and lost two others. We had three double hook-ups and managed to survive several near collisions with rocks, other boats, and massive waves.

That day stands out as one of the most exciting days of my life. The fishing was extraordinary, the scenery was stunning, and thrills were simply beyond description. When I think of the moments of fun, the serious danger and the efforts we went through, I still get tears in my eyes. I'm happy I turned the car around.

ANOTHER SEASON

The following year, we were back in Ucluelet with friends Jack Gunter and Carla Matzke. Jack and I fished the first day, and we rotated fishing companions for the rest of the week. An hour into the first day of fishing, my line went tight. It was a mighty tug, and line peeled violently off the reel. Jack and the guide retrieved the second pole and both downriggers.

After several years of battling king salmon, I came to the realization that it is best to let them have their way during the initial battle, letting the pole do the work without putting excessive tension on the equipment or fish. They can't go anywhere, and if they're hooked properly, they'll just run.

I had come to use this passive approach to claim victory over the mighty king on numerous occasions. As more line peeled off, I stood my ground and held the rod tip high. Once the fish slowed down and took no more line, I began to reel. The fish fought with honor and violence, but I knew in the long run, I would

SALMON FISHERMAN RETURNING WITH HIS PRIZE CATCHES.

RALPH AND MICHELE KYLLOE AND WELL-KNOWN WEST COAST ARTISTS JACK GUNTER AND KARLA MATZKE PROUDLY SHOW OFF THEIR MORNING'S CATCH FROM THE WEST COAST OF VANCOUVER ISLAND.

win. Just as I had relaxed and visualized the fish on board, he made a mighty run, and line tore from the reel. Moments later, the line went slack, and I realized that the fifty-pound line we were using had snapped under the weight of his pull. Those things happen, and with a bit of sadness in my heart, I helped the guide retie the line and rig the downriggers for a continuation of the day's fishing.

All went well throughout the rest of the day, and each of us caught our limit of kings and a few cohos that would be shortly sent to the smokehouse. Everyone has lost fish, and during the evening, my friends and I talked of the mighty battles, the adventures and disappointments of lost struggles.

The following morning we were fishing with a different guide but on the same boat. Within an hour of being on the ocean, my line went tight. I set the hook and knew from the weight of the pull that I had another king on the line. The fish fought with initial power and determination, and within ten minutes I had the fish in the guide's net. As we hoisted the fish on board, we noticed that my hook was not set where it should be. In fact it was not in the fish at all. What had happened was that it had become tangled in another flasher the fish was dragging behind him. It also became apparent that this was the fish that I had lost the day before. We radioed the guide who had taken us out on the prior day, and he confirmed that it was indeed his flasher that we had just taken from the fish.

Needless to say, the experience was the talk of the town that evening. The odds of ever finding the same fish out of thousands of square miles of ocean seems quite amazing. On top of that, my snagging the fish only added to the uniqueness of the experience.

A WATER VIEW OF THE ISLAND PRINCESS RESORT IN UCLUELET, VANCOUVER.

THE CAMPBELL RIVER

There is no more famous or exciting salmon river than the Campbell on the eastern shores of Vancouver Island. The water is clean and swift. Huge old trees line the banks and graciously shade the river with their strong limbs. On a memorable day in August of 1995, my wife and I decided to see and experience, close-up, the mysteries of the river that has so enchanted visitors for generations.

On that warm afternoon, we rented wet suits, masks, snorkels, and fins and ventured a few miles upstream of where the river meets the cold waters of the Pacific Ocean.

From the start, I should mention that I have an instructor's rating in whitewater canoeing. I have battled mighty rapids in an open boat and felt quite comfortable in my ability to navigate forceful waters, but upon our venture into the waters of the Campbell River, I knew immediately that I was significantly out of my element. Initially, it was one of the most humbling and exhausting experiences I had involved myself in as an adult. Fortunately, wet suits are buoyant and kept both of us on the surface. But the viciousness of the water smashed us into rocks and wrapped us around huge boulders that lay in wait to torment and punish us for our intrusion into the kingdom of water. I flailed out in agony as I was thrown against stones, and I withered in pain while trying to control my direction as we were pushed, uncaringly,

A BRIGHTLY PAINTED CANOE, IN THE TRADITION OF THE NORTHWESTERN COASTAL INDIANS, IS OFTEN USED IN FISHING FOR STEELHEAD TROUT IN WATERS NOT ACCESSIBLE BY ROAD.

STYLISH-LOOKING
FLY FISHERMEN
TRY THEIR LUCK IN
THE CAMPBELL
RIVER. THEY
LANDED A FISH ON
EVERY OTHER
CAST.

downstream by the rapidly descending waters.

Finally, I hit a small, calm, deep spot in the waters. As I looked down, I was awestruck at the sight below me and only a few feet away. Within reach of my hands were hundreds of monster salmon living their lives in majesty and hearing the calls that compelled them to return to the grounds of their birth. It is a calling that humans cannot comprehend. To realize that these fish had traveled thousands of miles and had lived four or five years in the vastness of the ocean only to find their way back to an obscure spot on some unknown river, can only remind humans of our insignificant understanding of the mysteries of the universe and of life itself.

As I traveled farther downstream, I saw fish that were beginning to age. Their humps, coloring, and hooked jaws told me that they were preparing for the final callings in their lives. Soon their individual efforts would be over and new life would continue. Their broken and discolored bodies would shortly nourish other forms of life. The dignity of the individual would be gone, and I could only hope that before they died, somewhere, in the back of their brains, they realized how magnificent they really were.

On that day, I saw probably thousands of fish, each remarkable in its own way. I also saw eagles and ospreys, watching intently from the branches of strong trees, who no doubt wondered what sort of creature was floating by them. Around a bend in the river, I spotted a mother black bear and a yearling cub looking for a meal. I was pleased that I was on the far side of the river. As I neared the mouth of the river, seals shot by me like torpedoes as they snatched an occasional unsuspecting salmon. In the bay, sea lions and killer whales kept watch for slow-moving fish that would, no doubt, make a tasty meal. From both tiny and

THIS BILLBOARD OF ADVERTISING RELATES TO THE FISHING COMMUNITY ON VANCOUVER ISLAND.

A HAPPY FISHERMAN WITH FOUR "PINKIES" CAUGHT OFF CAMPBELL RIVER.

more than three hours and had caught nothing. Then, without warning and much to my delight, my line ripped from the reel. The other line was retrieved and both the downriggers were raised from their depths. The line continued to peel. It finally slowed after several exciting seconds, and I noticed that almost all of the line had been taken from the reel. I started pumping the rod and in time had the a monster coho salmon near the boat and within easy eyesight. However, the second the fish caught sight of us, she turned and made her way a good hundred yards from the boat. With that run, we realized that this was no ordinary coho.

After significant effort, I once again had the fish near the boat, but everyone on the deck felt that the fish was not ready to surrender. Moments later, she peeled off another fifty yards of line, and after another effort on my part, I had her once again by the boat, where she again ran just about the full length of line on the reel.

On that day, she made five complete runs and took at least fifty yards of line on each run. Finally, technology prevailed, and she succumbed to the powers of something foreign and much stronger than herself. As we pulled her onto the boat, I could only respect her efforts and her desire to live and to complete her final calling. To die on a boat would have been, for her, as for most fish, an indignity. I wanted her to spread her genes throughout the entire ocean.

The loss of this fish was probably insignificant in the realm of the life as a whole. But good genes should not be wasted. I gently removed the hook from her now-limp body and carefully set her back in the water. I thought for a moment she might disappear from the surface with a mighty twist of her tail. Unfortunately, she turned belly up and no

huge boats, humans harvested salmon by the hundreds, a gift to the continuity of life.

Within time, I came to master the art of running rivers in a wet suit. It was completely necessary to keep my body perfectly flat and allow the river to take me where it wanted me to go. Fighting the river was worthless; it would always win and think nothing of it. It was not a challenge to the river to see if it could defeat an intruder. The river had a life of its own and did what it was supposed to do regardless of my intrusion.

The pleasures of the afternoon far outweighed the bruises and indignities I had suffered, and I realized again that life would go on at all costs. I was but an insignificant and temporary visitor to the home of the fish. They had lived and survived through millions of generations; they knew what they needed to know in order to survive.

FURTHER ADVENTURES

Our final day of fishing for the season found us once again trolling off the western coast of Vancouver Island. We had trolled for

LANDING A BIG ONE
IS A TWO-PERSON
JOB OFF THE
OCCASIONALLY
CROWDED COAST OF
VANCOUVER ISLAND.

THE TOWN SIGN AT
UNION BAY,
VANCOUVER
ISLAND. THE
ENTIRE COMMUNITY
IS GEARED TOWARD
FISHERMEN.

**A TROUT STREAM
ON VANCOUVER
ISLAND.**

amount of resuscitation would revive her. I eventually pulled her lifeless body back in the boat. She weighed nineteen pounds, large for a coho salmon.

This experience reminded me that life, regardless of what form it takes, needs to be respected. I have always felt that animals are not ours to slaughter for enjoyment. If I was going to kill something, I had a moral responsibility to eat it. Behind the efforts of every individual should be a basic and immovable respect for life, regardless of what form it may take.

THE CAMPS
APRIL POINT LODGE

Started in the 1950s, April Point Lodge has been owned and operated by the Peterson family for more than forty years. Located on Quadra Island, just across the bay from the town of Campbell River, the lodge occupies a small peninsula with world-class scenery. Mother Phyllis oversees the lodge and brothers Eric and Warren operate the facility on a day-to-day basis.

Not only do the Petersons offer extraordinary fishing with exceptional guides and a fleet of modern high-tech boats, but they provide a full range of related activities as well. If the fishing doesn't interest visitors, they may want to try sea kayaking or a visit to the local petroglyphs for a taste of history. They could also set out for a helicopter ride or a nature excursion that will offer sightings of killer whales, sea lions, eagles, and wildlife of all sorts.

The facilities at the lodge are unique. One can rent an ocean-front cabin with fireplace and hot tub, a deluxe single room overlooking the harbor, or a spacious five-bedroom guest house. Also at the lodge, visitors will find complete conference facilities and a restaurant that will leave them intoxicated with the taste

WATER VIEW OF THE QUINTESSENTIAL APRIL POINT LODGE ON QUADRA ISLAND OFF THE COAST OF VANCOUVER ISLAND.

APRIL POINT'S SALMON CHOWDER

1 lb. salmon filet
2 Tbs. butter
1 carrot, peeled and cut into matchstick-size pieces
1 celery stalk, diced
2 to 3 potatoes, peeled and diced
5 C. fish stock
1/2 tsp. thyme
1 bay leaf
2 Tbs. tomato paste
1/4 C. minced parsley
1 Tbs. capers, minced
Sour cream, as needed for garnish

Remove any bones from salmon filet. Cut into half-inch cubes and set aside. In a heavy saucepan, melt butter over medium-low heat. Add carrot, celery, and potatoes. Cover, and allow vegetables to steam in their own juices for four or five minutes or until almost tender. Add stock, thyme, bay leaf; simmer for ten minutes. Remove bay leaf before adding salmon cubes and tomato paste. Let simmer an additional five minutes or until salmon begins to flake. Stir in parsley and minced capers. Serve hot with dollops of sour cream in the center. Makes four servings.

of fresh-caught salmon and world-class food.

The true spirit of April Point Lodge is not with its full-service marina or other amenities. The essence of the lodge comes with the people associated with the facility. The fishing guides are exceptionally knowledgeable and experienced, and they are well versed in the lore of the area. Once their charters are complete, they hang around and talk with the clients, telling great fish stories and other tales that fascinate the listener. Eric Peterson, one of the owners, is always the consummate host who runs the cookouts held nightly during the season.

An annual Women's Invitational Salmon Fishing Contest is held, and contestants come from around the world to engage in fishing and camaraderie. The owner's well-mannered Labrador retrievers mingle with the guests and are a welcome addition to the nightly campfires. Wild seals and sea lions hang out at the dock and perform their antics for anyone willing to pay attention to them. Office and dining staff are there to insure the comfort of

HAPPY WINNER OF THE LADIES' INVITATIONAL SALMON FISHING TOURNAMENT HELD ANNUALLY AT APRIL POINT LODGE.

ONE HAPPY FISHERMAN WITH A FORTY-FIVE-POUND KING SALMON CAUGHT IN THE BAY JUST OFF APRIL POINT LODGE.

their guests and offer frequent congratulations and smiles as happy fishermen proudly unload their day's catch. For a great, world-class, fishing experience, April Point Lodge is a place worth visiting.

April Point Lodge
P.O. Box 1
Campbell River, British Columbia
V9W 4Z9 Canada
(604) 285-2222
(604) 285-2411 (fax)

THE GUIDES AT
APRIL POINT LODGE
NEAR CAMPBELL
RIVER RELAXING
AFTER FINDING THE
"BIG ONES" FOR
THEIR CLIENTS.

THE CAMPBELL RIVER LODGE

Located directly on the Campbell River a few miles north of the town is the Campbell River Lodge. At first glance, the buildings appear to be unassuming. Once inside, however, the lodge presents itself as a magical kingdom of salmon-fishing delight. Full of relics, the lodge is one of the oldest and most historical fishing camps on the island.

Campbell River Lodge offers first-class accommodations, and their food is, without a doubt, first rate. On several occasions, I have had meals personally prepared from fish I had caught only hours before. Meals are served in either the rustic dining room or on the verandah overlooking the river. Eagles, seals, and jumping salmon are commonly seen from the lodge porches. The food is as spectacular as the view, and I heartily recommend the hollandaise sauce and the locally brewed beers.

The lodge is known for its cozy ambience. This is definitely an uncrowded place, so relaxation after a fight with a forty-pound salmon is possible. For aching muscles or further relaxation, spend some time in the hot tub. Most importantly, the staff is friendly, and the fishing guides know where to find fish.

Campbell River Lodge
1760 Island Highway
Campbell River, British Columbia
V9W 2E7 Canada
(800) 663-7212
(604) 287-7446

CERTAINLY THE LARGEST SCULPTURE OF A FISHERMAN, THIS MONUMENT IS CUT FROM A SINGLE DOUGLAS FIR AND MARKS THE ENTRANCE TO THE CAMPBELL RIVER LODGE.

TACKLE SHOP AND
DISPLAY AT THE
CAMPBELL RIVER
LODGE. THE LODGE
IS FULL OF ANTIQUE
FISHING
MEMORABILIA,
ARTWORK, AND
RUSTIC AMBIANCE.
THE FISHING IS
ALSO EXCEPTIONAL.

PAINTERS LODGE

Painters Lodge is certainly the largest of the fishing lodges in Campbell River. One of several fishing camps owned by Oak Bay Marine Group, the facility offers the most up-to-date and modern amenities in the area. The scenery is spectacular, and fishing in the Discovery Passage is an experience every fisherman should have. Painters Lodge offers a full-service experience, and facilities are available for individuals or corporate retreats. If visitors tire of fishing, they can spend time in the heated swimming pool or the hot tub. Other diversions include tennis and golf.

The lodge also offers an extraordinary buffet full of local delicacies, or visitors can dine in the Fireside Lounge or the Tyee Pub. I recommend sitting at an outdoor table to watch the occasional ocean liner cross through the passage on its way to Alaska. Now and then a killer whale cruises within a stone's throw of the docks that house a fleet of Boston Whalers. Also, seals and eagles can often be sighted. If the lodge scenery isn't enough, buses are provided for a trip to town to see the local sights.

Painters Lodge
Campbell River, British Columbia
Canada
(800) 663-7090

A GUIDE AND FISHERMAN FROM PAINTERS LODGE WITH THE AFTERNOON'S CATCH.

PAINTERS LODGE AS SEEN FROM THE OCEAN SIDE.

BOSTON WHALER BOATS LINED UP AT PAINTERS LODGE, READY TO TAKE HOPEFUL FISHERMEN OUT FOR THE EVENING BITE.

FISHERMEN AT
PAINTERS LODGE ON
THE CAMPBELL RIVER
SHOW OFF THEIR
MORNING CATCHES.

CANADIAN PRINCESS RESORT

On the other side of the island, in the town of Ucluelet, the Oak Bay Marine Group also owns the Canadian Princess Resort. A rather extraordinary facility, guests are invited to stay in a traditional room on land, or they may prefer to sleep aboard a fully rigged 235-foot ship that floats in the harbor.

Fishing is done on gang boats, or guests may charter a local guide for a more personal experience. Visitors may dine onboard the *Canadian Princess,* or they may visit any of several local restaurants in the area.

Canadian Princess Resort
Ucluelet, British Columbia
Canada
(800) 633-7090

THE ISLAND PRINCESS, LOCATED IN UCLUELET, VANCOUVER ISLAND, HOUSES GUESTS IN EITHER A MOORED OCEANGOING VESSEL OR IN ROOMS LOCATED ONSHORE.

ISLAND WEST RESORT

Also in Ucluelet is the Island West Resort. This facility offers a complete guide service of modern boats to take fishermen onto the high seas for the thrill of a lifetime. If fishermen can't catch a monster salmon in this part of the world, then they're not trying. Also at the resort is a complete bait and tackle shop with enough "hoochies" and anchovies to make the day unforgettable.

After a day on the water, guests can visit the upstairs Marine Pub for locally caught fresh fish that melt in the mouth. The resort offers clean, comfortable rooms with kitchenettes, laundry, and other amenities at reasonable prices. The people are great, the prices fair, and the fishing fantastic. However, those prone to motion sickness should see their local pharmacist before going out on the water. Also, a drive down to Tofino is worth the trip. It's a beautiful little town with numerous art galleries and interesting sights.

Island West Resort
Ucluelet, British Columbia
Canada
(604) 726-7515

FISHERMEN AT THIS ISLAND WEST FISHING RESORT CLEANING STATION TOSS REMAINS OF FISH OFF THE END OF THE PIER TO WAITING SEA LIONS AND BALD EAGLES.

**CLEANING STATION
AT ISLAND WEST
RESORT IN
UCLUELET,
VANCOUVER ISLAND.**

RIVERSIDE BED AND BREAKFAST

In central Vancouver Island, I found a small town completely oriented to the fishing experience. Port Alberni, about three hours north of Victoria, is complete with many docks and bait and tackle shops. Here the fish are plentiful. One of the most charming local bed and breakfasts is the Riverside Bed and Breakfast. Located a few miles outside of the town, the Riverside is situated directly on the scenic Somass River.

Riverside is a spectacular log cabin, surrounded with open fields, dense woods, and a river so productive that fish, such as steelhead trout, can be caught year-round from the locals' back doors. In the fall and spring, coho and king salmon limits can be caught in just a short time. Fishing is done from the shore in waders, or fishermen can just wander the shoreline, throwing either flies or spinnerbaits.

The inn offers a variety of packages, so plan to spend some time there as the food is not only tasty but as plentiful as the fish. Prices range from $50 Canadian for a room to $120 Canadian for complete packages with all meals included. Knowledgeable local guides are available. The facility is located significantly off the road and is the favorite for sophisticated European and Oriental fishermen. Hence, reservations should be made early and can be scheduled around the local salmon festival and tournaments. One big fish can pay off a lucky winner's mortgage!

Riverside Bed and Breakfast
6150 Ferguson Road
Port Alberni, B.C. V9Y 7L5
CANADA
(602) 723-3474

THE PICTURESQUE
SALMON-FISHING
VILLAGE ON THE
SHORES OF
QUADRA ISLAND.

**TYEE BOATS AT
PAINTERS LODGE.**

CALIFORNIA

MANKA'S INVERNESS LODGE

Tucked in the hills of northern California, about an hour north of San Francisco, is the picturesque town of Inverness. There, just about ninety years ago, the Manka family built an oceanfront fishing camp. For many generations sportsmen thrilled at their impressive catches of salmon, halibut, abalone, and ocean-bottom fish. Numerous fresh-water fishermen also enjoyed the nearby rivers and streams as they filled their creels with delicate trout.

JUST AN HOUR NORTH OF MANKA'S INVERNESS LODGE, INVERNESS, CALIFORNIA, FISHERMEN LINE UP FOR THE FALL "PINKIE" SALMON RUN. IT'S NEARLY IMPOSSIBLE TO SEE A LIMP LINE WHEN THE FISH ARE RUNNING.

114

Manka's Inverness Lodge is surrounded today by 80,000 acres of National Seashore preservation land, rolling California hills, and lush vegetation. The lodge is a grand rustic lodge that speaks of times gone by. Full of antique fishing equipment and outdoor memorabilia, the inn is a statement of quality, quaintness, and hospitality. The extended wine cellar and gourmet menu, along with overly generous portions, ensure that guests are well satisfied. Fish of all sorts are caught in the harbor, brought to the kitchen, and prepared fresh for evening meals.

Each of the rooms in the main lodge is carefully decorated and preserved to maintain its rustic authenticity. Several small cabins that offer extraordinary ambiance to weary fishermen and guests who come just for a weekend getaway are also available.

Manka's Iverness Lodge is well known among the celebrities. On my weekend visit there, actor Sean Penn was in residence. He mingled politely, relaxing in the dining hall and visiting with other guests. That night, Penn and a friend stayed up late baking cookies. After breakfast in the morning, he shared the cookies with others who happened along.

Another celebrity of the lodge, though not as well known, is Louie, the oversized golden retriever. He is no doubt the friendliest dog on the planet, and if guests choose, they may bring their own best friends along; pets are welcome and will enjoy a long walk on the beach or chasing seagulls. This is one place where, even if a guest has no interest in fishing, he will thoroughly enjoy the stay anyway.

Rooms and cabins are available at rates between $85 and $265 per evening.

Manka's Inverness Lodge
P.O. Box 1110
Inverness, California 94937
(415) 669-1034

ONE OF SEVERAL CABINS AVAILABLE AT MANKA'S IVERNESS LODGE.

A BEDROOM IN A MANKA'S INVERNESS LODGE CABIN. MONSTER GOLDEN RETRIEVER LOUIE IS ON THE BED. LOUIE WILL BE HAPPY TO JOIN GUESTS FOR WALKS ON THE BEACH, OR GUESTS ARE INVITED TO BRING THEIR OWN PETS IF THEY SO CHOOSE.

THE DINING ROOM AT MANKA'S INVERNESS LODGE, WHICH WAS OPENED AS A FISHING CAMP IN 1917 AND TODAY OPERATES NOT ONLY AS A RESPITE FOR FISHERMEN BUT A WEEKEND GETAWAY FOR THOSE SEEKING ORIGINAL RUSTIC AMBIANCE, EXTRAORDINARY DINING, AND EXCEPTIONAL HOSPITALITY.

NOMENCLATURE

There is something wonderful about the human use of language. Humans are a creative lot, and given the opportunity, mountains of language grow exponentially as the complexity of a concept or activity grows. This is art at its finest. The broader and more intricate the concept, the more specifically language expands. Language is a creative process, and those with creative minds can use language to either totally confuse a listener or to create crystal clarity.

The field of medicine is a good example of how intricate language can become. It is nearly impossible for the layman to comprehend medical terminology. But to the trained physician, the more command of the language, the greater the understanding of the concept.

We fishermen are a creative and competitive lot, and we refuse to be outdone by engineers, physicians, lawyers, or other groups in their quest to be thought of as unique, professional, or even superior by their incessant use of language that nobody, other than themselves, can understand. Granted, some doctors, lawyers, and engineers are also fishermen. But, not to be forgotten, nor relegated to a position less than worthy, fishermen will not be outdone at the art of language.

I could take my doctor or lawyer friends moochin' with hootchies. Or maybe we'll go flippin' using Mister Twister Fightin' Crawdads with heavy action graphite rods strung with spiderwire. Or perhaps we'll check out the action with zug bugs or giant black stones, or we'll go jiggin'. Or maybe we'll throw some banana-scented, chartreuse powerworms rigged Texas style, or we'll use a gold, single-willow spinnerbait for nesting largemouths. Or we might even check out an Ausable Wolff or a Griffith Gnat on the spring run of steelheads.

We fishermen of the world can stand with our heads tall; we're just as good as the professional elites. While the rest of the world sleeps, we're out having the time of our lives. Few people are fortunate enough to say that!

A SERIOUSLY HAPPY PAIR OF "SPECK" FISHERMEN SHOW OFF THEIR MORNING'S CATCH.

A BAIT SHOP AND GUIDE SERVICE IN LAKEPORT, FLORIDA.

LARGEMOUTH BASS

Largemouth bass are nothing more than freshwater thugs. They're like hand grenades that explode almost immediately. They lie in wait for a victim, then they jump it with brutality and force. It's all over in less than a second. Many times, bass are caught with stomachs so full that they could not possibly eat more. They kill because of a mean temperament. Often, they attack lures just because they feel annoyed and irritated by the intrusion of a noisy object in their space.

A HAPPY BASS FISHERMAN IN FLORIDA.

Michele and I are serious bass fishermen. We have a modern bass boat with fish finders, trolling motor, live wells, and just about every accessory possible. Fishing almost daily during the season, we travel great distances throughout the year to spend time on water.

Certainly, our most memorable bass-fishing experience in the North came when we found ourselves in central Michigan on business with no boat and no tackle of any sort. We were lucky to stop in the state-forest area near Baldwin at the state's center. This area is known for spectacular trout and salmon fishing as well as for big muskies and northern pike.

On the evening of our arrival, we decided to spend an extra day fishing. So we went off to the local discount store and purchased a cheap rod and reel and a few spinnerbaits. We then spent the next few hours searching for a public boat dock or marina that would rent us

a boat. No luck. Finally, at about eleven at night, we stopped at an inexpensive-looking motel—Michele more aptly described it as "seedy"—on the side of the road and requested a room from the owner, who came to the front desk in her nightgown.

While checking in, I commented that we were disappointed in our inability to find a place to fish, so after renting us the room, the owner was kind enough to loan us an old aluminum rowboat that she kept on a small pond a few miles away. At daybreak, we found the boat and pond down a long dirt road full of bumps and potholes. It was pouring rain, but we decided to take our chances anyway.

The boat had not been used in years, and the only oars we found had broken oarlocks. Without fanfare, I pushed the boat from the muddy banks and began rowing, albeit awkwardly, to a lowland area about fifty yards away. The pond itself was probably about three acres and was surrounded on three sides with inexpensive ranch homes, a trailer park, and a swamp at one end—in truth, not a very picturesque lake.

My first cast landed near an overhanging tree, and the lure, unfortunately, became lodged on a submerged root. The first jerk to dislodge the spinner bait snapped my pole in half, ending any hopes of fishing that day. That was it. It was over and I began rowing back to the banks of the owner's cottage.

However, as I was rowing, Michele reconfigured the pole by retying the line and eliminating the broken top section. As we approached the bank she threw the lure into a small weedy area and was quite surprised when it was attacked by a bass. She instantly set the hook and retrieved a four-pound bass after an exciting fight. We both looked at each other, and I changed course to try another area a few feet away. Seconds later it was my turn.

Casting with a three-foot rod is not easy, and the most distance I could get was probably twenty feet from the boat. This was not, under any circumstance, a deep lake, but within a second of the lure being in the water, I had a strike and another large bass in the boat.

During the next two hours, the rain intensified and began to fill the boat. Without rain gear, we were both soaked. The air was cool, in the sixties, but the water in the lake was warm. By switching off rowing we were able to maintain body temperature, and although soaked to the bone, we were comfortable. The water in the lake was crystal clear, and the raindrops did not dampen our visibility or our outlook.

There is something awe-inspiring about nature. Nature knows no pity or sorrow. It only knows persistence and survival. To watch a largemouth bass explode from behind a sunken tree only a few feet away and see it attack a lure with its huge mouth gaping leaves a fisherman with a profound sense of both respect and fear.

Big bass fight differently than small bass. Pulling in a big bass is like pulling in an old tire. Small bass twist and turn and roll and fight for their lives.

On that day, we caught fifteen largemouth bass that weighed between three and seven pounds each, in less than two hours, using a broken rod and fishing from a leaking

A PICTURESQUE FLORIDA LANDSCAPE.

rowboat with broken oarlocks. We had no fish finder; we found them around tree stumps and weed beds, under docks and other boats moored to old pilings. I caught my largest behind an old, partially submerged fifty-gallon drum. In one shallow area only a few inches deep, my wife threw the lure about twenty feet from the boat and slowly retrieved the lure, keeping it just on the surface. About fifty feet away, a bass burst from under a lily pad and sped like a torpedo toward the lure. The water churned just a few feet from the boat, and we watched in awe as the bass brutally engulfed the lure with a mouth almost large enough to swallow a bowling ball. It was an inspiring sight.

Bass fishing in the northern states is exceptional and exciting. But because of the short growing seasons, the bass do not grow to the monster sizes of their humongous cousins in Florida. On many occasions, especially in the spring, Michele and I have caught as many as seventy-five bass in a day. But they usually range between one and three pounds.

Because of the unusual circumstances and the sizes of the fish, that day stands out as the most fun we ever had fishing for bass in the North. Once we pulled the boat from the lake, we jumped into our truck and returned to the motel room for showers and dry clothes. While we were checking out of the motel, the owner asked how the fishing was. I wanted to tell her about the fish. I wanted to tell her about the explosions and the battles and the clear water. I wanted to show her the joy we had experienced. But, I thought, forget it. I wanted that experience again, and if others knew of the pond, there would be nothing left within a few days. "Well," I said, "we didn't catch any fish and it was quite cold."

"Must have been the rain," she said. "Besides, nobody ever catches anything in that pond anyway. Next time you're in town I'll tell you where the locals fish."

"Great," I said as we left the office. I can't wait to find the good fishing spots in her area.

FLORIDA

For lovers of bass fishing, Florida is heaven. No doubt about it. Take my word for it. Many lakes and rivers in Florida are full of bass big enough to swallow a respectable cat. Certainly, the most famous is Lake Okeechobee in south-central Florida.

Lake Okeechobee is a legendary lake. Fishermen who have never fished the lake are missing one of the world's greatest fishing experiences. The past decade has brought significant pressure on the quantity and quality of fish, but the lake is so large that it is probably impossible to deplete the resources. Further, with the strong catch-and-release effort that is widely practiced today, the fishing should remain strong.

The real treat of Okeechobee is not necessarily the fishing. Words are not adequate to

SIGNS ADVERTISE THE FISHING EXPERIENCE IN CENTRAL FLORIDA. MOST OF THE LOCAL ECONOMY AND COMMUNITY AROUND LAKE OKEECHOBEE IS GEARED TOWARD THE FISHERMAN.

describe the natural beauty of the lake. The first time I fished the lake, I was with my seventy-five-year-old stepfather Albert Backus of Chicago. It was February, and we were having a brutal winter in New England. I called my family in Chicago, and Albert agreed to meet me in Miami the following week. I got a late-night flight and didn't arrive until midnight. We picked up a rental car and drove about five hours to the west side of Lake Okeechobee. We found our hotel and slept for a few hours before I picked up our boat.

As Albert was still sleeping, I made my way through the locks and on to the main body

MICHELE KYLLOE FISHING THE QUIET, SECLUDED BACKWATERS OF LAKE OKEECHOBEE.

of water for some midday fishing. Okeechobee is a wild lake. It closely resembles the Everglades and has miles and miles of swamps, weed beds, and floating islands. It is highly possible to get lost on the lake. I spent the first hour throwing spinner baits at obvious spots and marveled at the scenery. Not wishing to disturb the ambiance, I maintained myself quietly and stealthily approached spots of interest. I rounded a corner and was about ten feet from the shore when a crashing sound brought my heart to a full stop. There, flying right at me, was a full-grown alligator with mouth gaping and teeth slashing. The beast was no more then ten feet from me and charging. I immediately fell backwards to the bottom of the boat. The alligator splashed a foot or so from my boat and dove frantically under it into deeper waters. I watched him through clear waters as he glided past. No one told me there were alligators here. No one told me.

In retrospect, I'm certain that I simply startled him as he slept peacefully on the shore of his lake. I am also certain that he was not attacking me, but I guarantee that I will never swim or dangle my unprotected toes in any Florida waters. Since that incident, I have seen dozens of alligators in southern waters. Usually if startled, they charge for deep waters and scare the bejesus out of everything within earshot. Once in the water, they will lie quietly, and it is possible to see them lying on the bottom, safe and oblivious to the world above.

Since this experience, I've heard numerous alligator stories that would bring a smile to anyone's face. Unfortunately, the dangers are real and the stories often true. Along with the alligator danger, hordes of water moccasins inhabit southern waters, and once in a while, a fisherman might unexpectedly find one in his boat. One fellow I heard of used his machete to slash a snake in half. This also punctured a hole in his boat, allowing the boat to fill with water and leave him completely submerged in unfriendly waters. Another individual reached down to retrieve his lure and found a water moccasin on the end of his line. The snake quickly coiled himself around the poor fisherman's arm. Realizing his peril, the fisherman took out his knife and succeeded in hacking the creature to death. Probably not a pleasant experience for anyone, but, as the fisherman commented, "At least I got my lure back!"

Despite the alligator encounter, Albert and I fished out the week. Fishing was slow. We had hired a guide for a day, and even the catch from fishing with shiners was significantly off from the norm. Nonetheless, we had a great time and shared our stories with others for several years hence.

In recent years, I returned to Florida and had the opportunity to fish the "Big O" again. This time, Michele and I hired Tony Hussey of Okeechobee, to lead us to the waters of plenty. Tony is a patient man with an extraordinary understanding of the vast waters of Okeechobee. He came highly recommended

as one of the best guides on the lake. A few days prior to the start of our fishing, a major front came through, creating forty-mile-an-hour winds and dramatic temperature drops in both the air and the water. Guides across the lake canceled their charters, and everyone told us to rearrange our trip as no fish would be caught.

Tony, however, was not convinced, and we set off just after sunrise with four dozen

A BASS FISHERMAN UNLOADING AFTER A DAY ON THE WATER AT LAKE OKEECHOBEE, FLORIDA.

A STORAGE
FACILITY FOR BASS
BOATS AT
BUCKHEAD RIDGE
MARINA IN
OKEECHOBEE,
FLORIDA.

BASS-FISHING
GUIDE TONY
HUSSEY,
REGARDED AS ONE
OF THE BEST
GUIDES ON LAKE
OKEECHOBEE,
WILL CATCH FISH
WHEN NO ONE
ELSE CAN. (HE
USUALLY SMILES
MORE THAN THIS.)
ONCE AGAIN,
MICHELE KYLLOE
CAUGHT THE BIG
FISH OF THE DAY.

shiners, new sweatshirts from the local discount store, and hope in our hearts. At face value, fishing with shiners sounds boring. Each shiner costs about a dollar, and it is very easy to go through a hundred a day. But within the three-to-four hours of fishing, we landed thirty-five bass all above three pounds and many in the five-to-eight-pound range.

Alas, fishing with shiners is technical stuff and the rule of thumb is that if someone lands half of his strikes, he's doing very well. By day's end, we had well over a hundred strikes and landed not only big bass but pike, catfish, and mud fish. It was, in my book, one of the finest bass-fishing days we ever had. Tony, however, was not convinced. On a scale of one to ten, he gave the day a five. "No big fish," was his only response.

A good guide is a professional. Tony was the consummate. He told us fishing stories of the lake that helped the time go by between bites. I mentioned that I wanted to try fishing techniques other than shiners, and we practiced "flippin'" with Mister Twister Fighting Crawdads rigged Texas style, pitching with crankbaits, and throwing buzzbaits at floating hydrilla and water lettuce. Although I was quite comfortable with these techniques, I learned something new about each one with Tony's suggestions. A good fishing guide will take the time to show his guidees how to do something correctly.

The real test of a good guide is whether he'll hand over his rod to his guidee with a significant fish on it. For a seasoned fisherman, this is hard to do. Nonetheless, each time Tony's bait was hit, he handed the rod to either Michele or me. Whenever someone hires a guide, it is important to ask different people who are the best guides in the area.

Later that trip, Michele and I had the opportunity to fish several of the well-known bass lakes in the Orlando area. For our first day fishing, we hired guide John Leech of the Central Florida Guide Service. He arranged a room for us the night before, and we met him significantly prior to daybreak for coffee. A half hour later, we were launching at Overstreet Landing on Lake Kissimmee. For the past several years, the lake had become overgrown and was presently in the process of being drawn down to kill off excess vegetation.

At safelight, about six A.M., we made our way onto the waters with only a few other boats present. As the huge sun rose over the shores, the fish started hitting our shiners. One right after another, our bobbers disappeared below the surface as the swirls from attacking bass left the telltale marks of their presence. I missed my first five strikes, and Michele landed her first five. Not a good start for me, since we are comically competitive with each other. In time, however, I got the hang of it. My mistake was engaging the reel too early, trying to set the hook before the fish had the bait in place. At the end of the day, we had spent another hundred dollars on shiners but had landed about forty fish on at least twice that many strikes.

A PAIR OF LOCAL FISHING BUDDIES SHOW OFF THE FRUITS OF THEIR EFFORTS ON CENTRAL FLORIDA'S LAKE KISSIMMEE.

UNDER THE COACHING AND DIRECTION OF FISHING GUIDE TONY HUSSEY, MICHELE KYLLOE BATTLES WITH AN ELEVEN-POUND BASS THAT SHE LANDED.

pressure went through the roof with each new bird explosion happening just a few feet from the boat. In time, however, the noises of the environment proved to be captivating, and we marveled at the capacity of nature to produce so many variations of waterfowl. The lakes of Florida are a treasure to be shared by all and preserved for future generations.

The following morning Michele and I returned to the lake for more fishing. It was a Saturday morning, and we were surprised to see numerous boats either in the water or waiting to be launched. Once we'd purchased shiners, we realized that a tournament was about to start. Without hesitation, I paid the entry fee and discussed the rules with the chairman. It was to be a half-day tournament with weigh-in at noon. So at safelight we charged onto the lake with the other boats to seek "the big one."

Around eleven-thirty, we noticed several other boats returning and made our way back to the docks for the weigh-in. Throughout the morning I had caught and released a few small bass and produced, unfortunately, nothing to be weighed by the chairman. Michele,

FISHING CAMP SIGNS FOUND IN FLORIDA.

John Leech was the consummate host and guide, dazzling us with his ability to pick spots from huge fields of lily pads that produced fish as soon as the shiners or artificial lures hit the water.

Like all other lakes in Florida, Lake Kissimmee is the habitat of endless forms of wildlife. As one fishes the shores of these lakes, ducks and other birds explode from their hiding places in the weeds. Considering my earlier experience with the alligator, my blood

THIS BAIT SHOP AND FISHING-TACKLE FACILITY IS IN FLORIDA'S BASS COUNTRY.

however, weighed in with her limit and won her category with eighteen pounds, her biggest fish being seven pounds. It was interesting, however, as she stood in line for her turn at the scales. The official asked what boat she was with, and she responded by giving the name I registered under. He smiled at her, and asked if she caught anything. Her reply, with a twinkle in her eye, was simply, "I caught all of them"

"Oh," was his only comment as he read the scales. The winner of the tournament won with twenty-four pounds and a ten-pounder to take first prize.

It was a thrilling morning, and I often have to listen to Michele as she tells of her victory over me to our fishing friends. She has also, on several occasions, mentioned that her defeat over me was payment for my stealing a salmon from her on our first visit to Vancouver Island.

THE CAMPS

There are literally hundreds of fishing camps in Florida. Many are nothing more than trailer parks where individuals may park their recreational vehicle and fish inexpensively for a few days. Others offer either a room or cabin, a bait shop, and a boat launch all for set fees. Still others cater to the specific needs of the bass fisherman and offer high-style living to those willing to pay the price. It is advisable to get recommendations from others who have stayed at certain camps before signing up for a week of relaxing in the sun. It is also advisable to make reservations significantly in advance because the best spots are reserved as much as a year in advance. It is also critical when booking any fishing vacation to ask the local bait shop owner, guide, or motel owner when is the best time of the year to go fishing in the area.

THIS HAPPY FISHERMAN SHOWS OFF HIS CATCH AT A BASS TOURNAMENT IN FLORIDA.

PICTURED IS AN OUTSIDE VIEW OF THE BASS HAVEN LODGE AND THE ST. JOHNS RIVER IN FLORIDA.

131

BASS HAVEN LODGE

Located on the St. Johns River two hours west of Orlando, the Bass Haven Lodge is one of the premier fishing camps of the area. Accommodating up to twenty-five guests at a time, the camp maintains several small brick cabins that come with kitchenettes and heaters. Boats with motors are available at the lodge, as are fishing guides. The well-groomed lawns and the soaring oak trees covered with Spanish moss are picturesque and inviting for a relaxing afternoon, or for weary muscles tired from pulling in big fish, guests may spend an evening soaking in the hot tub overlooking the spectacular river.

Certainly one of the best amenities of the lodge is the dining. First-class food is served to those staying at the lodge as well as those who travel great distances to enjoy the plentiful meals. The Hootens, the present owners, are all characters themselves and are known for their interesting stories of the area. The cabins are clean and exceptionally well maintained. A variety of friendly cats reside at the camp, and guests are welcome to invite these overly friendly creatures into their rooms for an evening's stay. The prices for the cabins range between $40 and $70 per night.

Bass Haven Lodge
P.O. Box 458
Welala, Florida 32193-0458
(904) 467-8812

THE BASS HAVEN
LODGE ON FLORIDA'S
ST. JOHNS RIVER IS
NOT ONLY WELL
KNOWN AS AN
EXCELLENT FISHING
FACILITY BUT
LOCALS COME FROM
MILES AROUND TO
ENJOY THE FOOD
SERVED IN THE
RESTAURANT.

LAKE MARIAN PARADISE

The Lake Marian Paradise Park is a relaxed and unassuming facility that caters to both senior citizens and the younger sportsman. On our visit to the camp, we were surprised by the large number of storks resting on the lawn. We then realized the reason for their visit. Two very successful fishermen were cleaning their day's catch of more than a hundred crappies (also called specks) in the cleaning station. Once each was cleaned, the fisherman tossed the remains into one of the canals, and a swarm of storks descended for an evening meal. Lake Marian is one of the Florida lakes that receives significantly less pressure than its better-known cousins. Consequently, the fishing is superb for both panfish and big bass.

The lodge maintains both efficiency rentals and hookups for recreational vehicles. Many retired individuals have enjoyed the facility so much that they have purchased adjoining lots, built homes, and become permanent residents. The grounds are well manicured, and the buildings are exceptionally well maintained and clean. Along with accommodations, the campground offers a bait and tackle shop, boat and motor rentals, and a laundry.

For a real treat, just a block or so away is the Lake Marian Restaurant that carries some of the best fresh-caught catfish in the state. I have stopped in several times over the years, and the people associated with the lodge are friendly, polite, and genuinely interested in others; they are more than willing to share their stories.

Motel units with kitchenettes range from $40 per day to $750 for the month. Recreational-vehicle hookups are $16.50 per day including boat slip.

A HAPPY RETIRED COUPLE AT LAKE MARIAN PARADISE LODGE, WHO SPEND THEIR WINTERS AT THE CAMP, OFFERED SOME OF THE BEST FISH RECIPES WE EVER TASTED.

Lake Marian Paradise
    Recreational Vehicle Park
901 Arnold Road
Kenansville, Florida 34739
(407) 436-1464

LAKE MARIAN PARADISE ON LAKE MARIAN, KENANSVILLE, FLORIDA, A SMALL UNASSUMING BODY OF WATER THAT IS A HAVEN FOR SERIOUS "SPECK" FISHERMAN AS WELL AS THOSE WHO LIKE AN OCCASIONAL "TACKLE BUSTIN'" BIG BASS.

CALUSA LODGE

Those who like a rugged, rustic atmosphere will love the Calusa Lodge. Located on the western shores of famous Lake Okeechobee in the sleepy town of Lakeport, Florida, the Calusa Lodge is steeped in history and tradition. The facility was opened sometime in the 1940s, and additions have been added throughout the years.

Along with providing rooms and recreational-vehicle hookups, the lodge offers one of the finest sportsmen's restaurants in the South. On the walls are dozens of mounted trophy bass, alligators, ducks, and freshwater fish of every variety. After a hard day on the water, relax with a beer and appetizers of alligator, frog legs, catfish, or turtle. Another option is to enjoy a full buffet of regional delicacies. Breakfast starts at 5:30 A.M. and dinner is served until 9:30 P.M. In the evenings, the bar is a meeting place for several local guides, and conversations across tables are common. Guests can be prepared for some great fishing tales, and they are encouraged to join in the conversation.

Calusa Lodge offers no pretensions of luxury. Those wanting beauty facilities will find that this is not the place. But if looking around, guests might see such notables as actor Don Johnson, Hank Williams Jr., Dickie Betts of the Allman Brothers Band, and numerous other celebrities who often frequent the lodge. In general, rooms range between $35 and $45 per night, and some have kitchenettes. Many spots for recreational vehicles and boat slips are also available.

In addition, Calusa Lodge operates a full-service bait and tackle shop, and Frank Garrison runs the Native Guide Service for some of the best fishing in the world.

Calusa Lodge
Route 2
Lakeport, Florida 33471
(941) 946-0544

MICHELE KYLLOE
FISHING THE
QUIET, SECLUDED
BACKWATERS OF
LAKE
OKEECHOBEE.

MOSSY COVE FISHING RESORT

Located on Lake Istokpoka in Lorida, Florida, Mossy Cove Fishing Resort is one of many unknown and secluded fishing camps that speaks of rustic flavor and ambiance. Small and unpretentious, the camp offers cabins, recreational-vehicle hookups, a small bait shop, and a boat ramp.

In the evenings, many of the guests get together at a covered pavilion overlooking the lake and cook their daily catch. A warm and personal place, Mossy Cove lives up to its name because it is shaded by towering oak trees that are covered with Spanish moss. The camp offers a firsthand opportunity to see wildlife up close and to experience some of the best fishing the country has to offer.

For an out-of-the-way fishing experience, guests should spend some time on Lake Istokpoka, and when they show photos of the huge fish they caught, they shouldn't tell anyone where they caught them. Hopefully, the camp and lake will go unspoiled for many years in the future.

Mossy Cove Fishing Resort
Lorida, Florida
(813) 655-0119
(800) 833-2683

A MOSS-COVERED TRAIL LEADS TO THE LAKE AND BOAT DOCKS AT MOSSY COVE FISHING RESORT.

CABINS AT MOSSY COVE
FISHING RESORT ON LAKE
ISTOKPOKA ARE NOTHING
FANCY, BUT THE PLENTIFUL
FISH, FRIENDLY PEOPLE,
ALLIGATORS, AND VAST
ARRAY OF WILDLIFE MAKE
THE RESORT WELL WORTH
THE TRIP.

ANGLERS MARINA

Anglers Marina, on the southern shores of Lake Okeechobee, is a world-class fishing resort. The base for many fishing tournaments, Anglers Marina offers a full-service marina capable of repairing boats or selling custom-fitted boats that would make even the most sophisticated of bass pros proud. Their tackle shop is well stocked with up-to-date equipment and people who know how to use it. They also sell shiners and provide a guide service for first timers and advanced fishermen as well. The resort also offers an inexpensive dockside efficiency motel, deluxe high-end waterside condos for rent, complete recreational-vehicle hookups and covered and uncovered boat slips.

My first experience with Anglers was when my brand new bass boat broke down on its maiden voyage to Florida. A two-dollar part prevented the boat from advancing into gear, and although Anglers did not have the part, they called every other dealer in Florida to try to locate the damn thing—to no avail; the piece had to be shipped from Atlanta. Nonetheless, they made a great effort to have me back on the water as soon as possible.

Apart from the top-notch facility, the people there are great. Warm and friendly, they go out of their way to ensure that their guests' stay with them is exceptional. Those wanting to hear great fishing stories should make sure to spend some time with reservationist Gussy Pitts. She'll tell all about the alligators and the water moccasins, and where the big fish are. She's worth the visit.

Anglers Marina
910 Okeechobee Boulevard
Clewiston, Florida 33440
(800) 741-3141

ON THE SHORES OF LAKE OKEECHOBEE, FLORIDA, ANGLERS MARINA PROVIDES COVERED BOAT DOCKS AS WELL AS EXPERIENCED GUIDES WHO KNOW THE FLORIDA WATER.

ANGLERS MARINA IN CLEWISTON,
FLORIDA, ONE OF THE FINEST
FACILITIES IN THE STATE, OFFERS
INEXPENSIVE MOTEL RATES AS WELL
AS VERY HIGH-END CONDOS FOR
EXTENDED STAYS.

FISH STORIES

The world is replete with stories. Human folklore and legends define us and help make us who we are. Further, there is the human propensity to exaggerate and suggest that things were a bit more extreme than they really were. It makes us feel important, and under many circumstances a bit of exaggeration adds to the uniqueness and interest of any event. Most of us try to depict an experience accurately, but often many fall prey to the temptations of exaggeration and, ultimately, embellish the specific details of their experiences.

AUTHOR AND BASS-FISHING GUIDE FROM THE ADIRONDACKS RALPH KYLLOE WHO CAUGHT AND HAPPILY SHOWS OFF THE LARGEST AND HEAVIEST BASS EVER CAUGHT IN LAKE OKEECHOBEE.

A 1950S SIGN LOCATED ON THE SIDE OF A MARINA ON VANCOUVER ISLAND.

BAYSHORE
MOTEL
Pacific Sunrise
COMPLETE KITCHEN UNITS PHONE
RELIABLE
SEA SIDE 726-4624
FULL CHARTER SERVICES PROVIDED
RESERVATIONS PH- Island West Resort
SHARP/72

ALTHOUGH BASS
WORLD LODGE, AS
SEEN HERE FROM
THE ST. JOHNS
RIVER, IS A SMALL
FACILITY, THE
CAMP OFFERS A
WELL-STOCKED
BAIT AND TACKLE
SHOP, AN
EXCELLENT GUIDE
SERVICE, AND A
CHARMING OWNER
WHO IS FULL OF
ENTERTAINING
STORIES.

Fishermen, on the other hand, love to embellish every detail of everything that ever happened to them. We are not born liars. That's too negative a term. We just love to tell stories, and with each new telling the facts become bolder. For instance, two fishermen are sitting at a table, and one says that no boys and very few men could have caught this fish; the other fisherman comments that the fish was so big that just the photograph weighed seven pounds. In essence, this proclivity is harmless. Other fishermen know this and usually join in the fun and enjoyment of a good yarn. Unfortunately, some nonfishermen fail to see the pleasure derived in the telling of a good story and have labeled any tale told by a fisherman as a "fish story." This is unfortunate but again reasonably harmless. Nonetheless, my heart goes out to the poor individual who cannot revel in the joys of a good fish story.

Over the years, good stories have spread throughout the fishing community, and I often wonder what the world would be like if such stories did not exist. In all honesty, the world would be a sterile place if we only presented ourselves in absolute facts and figures; the world is a better, far more interesting place because a few facts and figures were blown out of proportion.

Fishermen throughout the world are united in the thought that a bad day fishing is better than a great day at the office. We also believe that "life ain't worth livin' if ya can't go fishin'!" With these thoughts in mind, I recall the dying fisherman's last question to a priest before he passed away. "Father," he asked, "will there be fishing in heaven?"

The priest smiled. "Son," he said, "it wouldn't be heaven without fishing."